Profits Aren't Everything, They're the Only Thing

PROFITS

AREN'T

EVERYTHING,

THEY'RE THE

ONLY THING

**No-Nonsense Rules from the Ultimate
Contrarian and Small Business Guru**

GEORGE CLOUTIER

WITH SAMANTHA MARSHALL

HARPER
BUSINESS

An Imprint of HarperCollins*Publishers*
www.harpercollins.com

To the millions of small business owners who are the unsung heroes of our nation's economy.

Names and identifying details have been changed throughout to protect the privacy of the individuals whose stories are discussed in this book. The advice herein is for informational purposes only, and the author and publisher disclaim all liability for any losses that might be sustained as a result of following the information in this book.

FIRST EDITION

Designed by Eric Butler

Library of Congress Cataloging-in-Publication Data
    Cloutier, George.
        Profits Aren't Everything, They're the Only Thing : no-nonsense rules from
the ultimate contrarian and small business guru / George Cloutier. — 1st ed.
            p.   cm.
        ISBN 978-0-06-183285-7
    1. Small business—Management. 2. Profit. 3. Success in business. I. Title.
    HD62.7.C59   2009
    658.02'2—dc22   2009013605

09   10   11   12   13   OV/RRD   10   9   8   7   6   5   4   3   2   1

Contents

Introduction

YOUR SALES ARE DOWN. Your operating costs are out of control. Your cash flow has slowed to a trickle. Your bank won't give you a loan. Of course you blame the economy. Everyone's suffering, so it's no wonder your business is in trouble. Right?

WRONG!

Don't blame the economy. Recession or no recession, if your small business is failing, *it's your fault!*

Sure, we all take hits in downturns. But if you're struggling, if you can't turn a profit no matter how hard you try, if you're slicing your salary or facing foreclosure, it's because you've been doing something wrong all along. Take a good hard look under the hood and you'll see that most of the problems in your small business are internal. But guess what? That's *good* news! That means the situation is not beyond your control. *It can be fixed!* And I'll show you how.

It won't be easy. I'm about to tell you some tough truths. Get ready. My advice is controversial and uncompromising. I won't flatter you, I won't humor you, and I'll never let you off the hook. Think of this book as a wake-up call that's long overdue.

My company, American Management Services, has been working to turn around Main Street businesses just like yours for almost three decades. There's nothing we haven't seen and we've rarely encountered a situation we couldn't fix by rolling up our sleeves and getting to the root of the problem. This book will give you the benefit of our collective wisdom and experience. But first, one important rule: *No more excuses!*

If you've picked up this book, you're probably already running your own small or midsized business or thinking about starting one. Maybe you're expanding and wondering about your next step. Maybe you're doing okay, but your competitors are doing better and you're wondering if you could be doing more to increase sales. Or maybe you're like hundreds of my clients, who suddenly find, along with everybody else, that the tide has turned and the ship of easy profits has long sailed. The hidden problems in your business aren't so secret anymore. All those tough decisions you've been shoving to the bottom of your "to do" list are finally glaring back at you, waiting to be made.

Whatever your unique situation, the next steps to take are all here in the pages that follow. But before you read on, you have to make a decision. You have to ask yourself, "Why am I in business? What's my goal?"

Your answer should be "to make profits."

Why get into business if not to make as much profit as you possibly can? If you just want to be comfortable, go find yourself a secure job where you can punch a clock, pick up a paycheck, and hope for a great pension. If you want to contribute to society, found a nonprofit organization. But, if entrepreneurship is in your blood, why not work for the most that you can get?

The truth is, one of the many reasons people go into business on their own is because they are not happy where they are. Few say they started a machinery shop or a hair salon because they wanted to be a billionaire. They just thought they could do it better than their bosses did, and they wanted to enjoy life a little more. But if you don't have the controls and processes in place, you're just going to put more weight onto your shoulders. Far from gaining more control over your own life, you lose it, and become a slave to the staff and vendors you have to pay to keep the business alive. But there's a solution to this, a way to regain control: put Profits First, *always*!

I'm not going to lie to you. Making a real profit takes unwavering dedication to your business. When I travel the country giving seminars sponsored by Partner America, a strategic alliance I co-founded with the U.S. Conference of Mayors to promote and develop small business, I have each member of the audience fill out a questionnaire. The most important question I ask them is this: "On a scale of 1 to 10, how hard do you work?" I get a lot of 8s and 9s. But I'm always amazed at how few people say 10. I tell them, if they didn't check off 10, they're not working hard enough. That's why they're not making money.

Challenge yourself to do better, even if it means coming in on Saturdays and Sundays. You can go fishing any weekend. But the time to make a profit is always now. Business is not complicated. It all boils down to how hard you work, and how smart you work, in good times and in bad. Do more. Get more. And be ruthless in your quest to make money.

I know it's rough out there. According to the latest numbers by the Small Business Association, more than a million businesses are expected to file for bankruptcy this year. We may well be in the midst of the worst recession any of us will ever live through and no one knows how long it will last, or how much harder it will hit.

I remember in May 2008, five months into the official start of the recession, when Council of Economic Advisors Chairman Edward Lazear said, "The data is pretty clear that we are *not* in a recession." Oops. Guess he was wrong. And economists are often wrong about what's really important to our nation's economy. Even though this nation's 23 million small businesses are the backbone of our regional and local economy, employing more than 60 million people, creating 70 percent of new jobs each year, and generating about half of our GDP, many economists have no clue about the realities that small businesses face.

What's been happening on Wall Street infuriates me. When I see how the big banks, and AIG, have been making money off your backs and giving out multimillion-dollar bonuses for sheer incompetence, I want to stand up and scream, "Why didn't you fire these people?!" I want to organize a Million Small Business Persons March on Washington to demand the impeachment of the incompetent bureaucrats, who were supposed to be overseeing our financial system. What's been happening on Wall Street and in our government is a disgrace! Washington should be putting controls on the billions in bailout money they've been giving companies that have flagrantly abused our trust. And the government should be giving you, the small business owner, access to loans at 2.26 percent, just like they've been giving the big finance houses. This country's small business owners create 74 percent of all the jobs in this country. It's your investment, your sweat, and your dedication that's going to get this nation back on its feet. Of course you should be getting more help!

It's a lousy picture, but one of the biggest dangers of an economic downturn is the excuse it gives small business leaders to lie down and do nothing. You can say to yourself, "Everybody else is struggling so I might as well go home at five and get in nine holes of golf before dinner." Or you can ask yourself, "Do I really want to commiserate with all the other losers on the ninth hole . . . or do I want to make a profit?"

Start with the basics. No one should know your financials better than you. Your balance sheet is something that is within your control. YOU are the best judge of how to handle your money, if you know the right things to do. And the first thing you should do is take stock of the profits coming in, and the cash flowing out. Know where you stand.

The second thing you should do is to pay close attention to what I have to say in this book. Be assured, I am right there in the trenches with you. I've been on the docks for clients, counting heads of lettuce to make sure none of the inventory gets stolen. I've done the graveyard shift at truck stops to make sure sticky fingers aren't taking cash from the till. There is no task too small or too unpleasant. At my firm, we do whatever it takes to get our clients back on track.

There is nothing I preach that I don't practice myself as a business owner. Day to day, I've made the same mistakes that you have. I am CEO of a multimillion-dollar company with 150 people on staff, and I know the pitfalls of managing employees, keeping cash flowing, and micromanaging every last detail of operations. It isn't easy. My company is in the top quartile in my industry. Most years we have achieved 20 percent profit growth, but we are far from perfect.

I've let my hand slip from the wheel, and I'll share some of these stories with you throughout the book.

But be assured, when we hit a trough at American Management Services, we get ourselves out fast, because we're always willing to ask ourselves the tough questions. Start now. Ask yourself:

Do you take responsibility for every aspect of your business?

Don't blame employees when they don't do something right. You're the boss. You're the one who has to make sure things go well. If something goes wrong, it's your fault. Make that your attitude and you'll start to see fewer and fewer mistakes. And if someone is making too many mistakes or isn't pulling their weight, let them go!

Do you love your business as much as your family?

You should. If your wife or child were in a crisis, wouldn't you do everything imaginable to help them out?

Do you play golf?

Stop. That's time you could be spending with the business.

Do you work on Sundays?

If not, why not? I know most people are off on Sundays, but you could be grabbing the business that others are losing because they're at home being lazy. Use the day to go on sales calls. Meet prospective clients or customers. Make your business grow.

Do your workers respect you?

I didn't say "LIKE" you. I said "RESPECT" you. Because if you're making money, they're making money, and money gets everyone's respect.

Are you aware of all of your customers and their needs?

As a CEO I want to know who called and when, what they wanted, what they bought, how we helped them, how we didn't, what they liked, and what they didn't. You must micromanage and then micromanage some more. With a small business you have to know everything that's going on at all times.

Does your ego get the best of you?

Never rest on yesterday's sales. You must try harder than yesterday and harder still tomorrow. Exorcise the ego.

Are you clear in your orders?

When you say something, say it with conviction and stand by it. YOU are the boss.

Do you pay for performance?

Money talks! Workers work better when they know they'll be rewarded. If someone does a good job, encourage it. If they do a bad job, punish them. Weed out the ones who are not serious about making your business as successful as it can be.

Do you pay yourself well?

Always pay yourself first. If you're not happy with your salary, you know there's more work to be done. Vendors don't care about you. They can wait for their money. They aren't going anywhere.

Are you a defeatist?

Never, EVER talk yourself into a negative position. It's easy to say; "Oh, the economy is down," "Everyone is hurting," or "I need a rest." If you find yourself making these excuses, it's time to work harder. You'll be surprised at the energy that comes when your hard work starts paying off.

Are you satisfied?

You shouldn't be. There's always some way to make things better. It's that little extra that makes the difference between just another struggling business and a resounding success. Failure isn't an option. Commit to doing whatever it takes. Decide how much profit you want to make. Focus on it. Don't wish for it or imagine what it would be like. Force it into reality. Fight for every sale. Learn to love winning.

You must do today what others won't, so you can achieve tomorrow what others can't. Do everything to take care of business and everything else will take care of itself. Work harder, faster, and smarter than the competition by a factor of ten. Then, and *only* then, when everyone else is on the golf course grumbling about how much business is down, can you have fingertip control of your business while you are on your yacht. Or in your mansion. Or driving your Rolls Royce.

Success is sweet. But how successful you become is up to you.

PROFITS AREN'T EVERYTHING,
THEY'RE THE ONLY THING

Profits Aren't Everything, They're the *Only* Thing!

ABOUT TWO YEARS AGO we were working with a masonry contractor in North Carolina who was out of cash. The owner was a decent, God-fearing, and hardworking fellow, but his back was against the wall and he couldn't even pay his taxes or his payroll.

I put Lou Mosca, our senior vice president for client operations, on the case. Lou, a no-nonsense kind of guy, looked at the client's list of receivables and saw hundreds of thousands of dollars in unpaid invoices owed to him. But one in particular was so large, it stood out. The contractor had done some work on the local church, the one he attends, and for months the pastor hadn't paid him. The church owed the contractor $50,000.

When Lou asked him why he hadn't collected, the guy replied, "It's my church, what can I do?"

"I'll show you what you can do. Get in the car," Lou said.

The two of them drove to the church, and the contractor sat quietly in a pew while Lou politely but firmly confronted the pastor. He collected $50,000 on the spot, and the pastor apologized.

From then on, employees at that company looked at us with awe. We'd collected from a man of the cloth and didn't get struck down by lightning. The cash flow generated by the paid receivables pumped new life into the business, which is thriving today. When the owner thanked us, Lou said:

"From God's hands to your checkbook, Lord willing, you've got to get paid."

The contractor had committed one of the biggest sins against business by failing to collect. But he found redemption, and profits, in the end.

Amen!

Shocked? Good! Because many of you need your own lightning bolt to jolt you awake. This book is about an attitude adjustment and the need for your total commitment to run over anyone or anything that gets in the way of your company's paramount need for *profits*. That's all you should care about. In fact, if you don't want to be in the top quartile of your business and you choose to wallow in mediocrity and failure, you should probably stop reading now.

Still with me? Great! That means you're ready to do anything and everything necessary to maximize your profits. Be ruthless in this quest. If you have to terminate family members, so be it. It's time to stop whining about the diminishing demand from the marketplace, employees who are not performing, or banks that won't extend your credit because you are losing money. It is in your power to maximize your profits, solve your problems, and have a good life. You have to decide whether you want to be a pillar of your community because you have a strong and well run company, or waste your time spinning yarns and fantasies to yourself about how well you're doing. It's in your hands now.

You can do it. The Profit Rules described in this book, honed over thirty years of direct experience, analysis, and implementation, will give you the razor edge you need to turn your business into a profit machine. Our experience with 6,000 small businesses, in over 300 industries, has allowed me to see firsthand what works and what you need to do, starting today. Our consultants have spent nearly one million hours on Main Street, from Bangor, Maine to Oakland, California. We have identified over $1 billion in additional profits for our clients. We've made real profits happen for every conceivable kind of business, from day spas, car dealers, and construction companies, to T-shirt and fire engine manufacturers and, even a lard producer (that was a slippery one). We've helped companies ranging in size from one-person proprietorships to 500-employee operations. We've worked shoulder to shoulder with owners suffering mediocre profits or on the brink of disaster. We've pulled thousands of businesses into profitable, sustainable enterprises that will endure.

I don't care how bad it looks. Any business can achieve profits when its owners have the right focus and drive.

Get Paid!

Many of the solutions are probably staring you in the face right now. Finding them is a matter of reordering your priorities and facing the truth about your financials.

Be honest with yourself. There are plenty of simple steps to get cash that I know you are not taking. Small businesses always have way too many outstanding bills on their books; too many customers who have yet to pony up. It's the most obvious way to get the cash flowing again, and it always amazes me how reluctant business owners are to ask their customers for the money owed to them. The story of that pious contractor is all too common. Why be shy about it? Collect, collect, collect!

I'M GOING TO GIVE IT TO YOU STRAIGHT: WHATEVER REASON YOU THINK YOU STARTED YOUR OWN BUSINESS, IT'S ALL ABOUT THE CASH.

Don't measure success by how many employees you have, how much you contribute to your local church, how big a boat you own, or even what your sales are. When it comes to determining the true health of a business, those aren't the measures that count. My company has 150 employees. So what? Show me how much money I have at the end of the month, and then I might get excited.

Profits Equal Cash

Paper profits for small business are meaningless and misleading. Small businesses can't afford not to have a steady cash flow. You have to run things with real numbers. There is no room for anything else. In small business, cash flow is king. It has to be. Payroll has to be met. Otherwise you'll have a group of angry employees ready to take you to court.

Do an estimated cash-based profit and loss statement each week. You should know where you are financially and adjust accordingly and aggressively. Cut, cut, and cut some more. Focus on cash flow and expenses right now. If money is tight or you foresee problems, be ruthless about slicing expenses, whether for payroll, rent, or travel expenses. If you have three useless employees, get rid of them. If the expense accounts are getting out of hand, set strict limits. There's always extra fat to trim.

You have to have ironclad fiscal discipline. Particularly in a down market, but even when the economy is robust, small business owners need to be aware of their financial positions at all times. When they start failing, the ship goes down fast (more on this later).

Tolerate No Excuses; Trample All Obstacles

We had a metal fabrication contractor in Wyoming two years ago making $10 million a year in sales and $800,000 in profit. But the company, owned by a husband and wife team, was broken. One day the wife, who handled all the accounts, called Lou into her office and told him their coffers were empty.

"Why?" asked Lou. "How can that be?"

"Mr. Mosca, it's a mess. I've got $3.5 million in receivables and the money just isn't coming in," she said. "Take a look for yourself."

She stepped away from her desk and invited Lou to look at the spreadsheet on her computer screen. It was a dog's breakfast. She had a gun to her head on a $4 million contract. She was dealing with change orders, money leaks, and late deliveries. She was broker than broke, and it didn't look like she'd be collecting on her invoices anytime soon.

The healthy profits on paper (cash is the only profit) masked a host of problems. The business lacked the internal controls it needed. It had problems executing projects and meeting deadlines. Major clients challenged the quality of the work. The husband made bids on contracts he wasn't qualified to handle. The wife blamed him for unrealistic estimates, poor purchasing procedures, and excessive overtime from workers.

We addressed all of these issues. We also found the business a saving of $75,000 on insurance costs. But the project ended. The husband wasn't willing to follow through on our recommendations. He just kept pointing to the balance sheet.

"Well, I don't know what your problem is. Look at these profits!" he said. "We must be doing something right!"

The rosy financial statement was allowing him to continue in his happy state of denial and make excuses all the way to bankruptcy court. (More in the next chapter on how deadly denial can be to your business.)

Accounting profit matters only if you manage it right and turn it into cash. Either way, you still have to pay taxes on it. When December 31 comes and you made $10 million in sales and $1 million in profit, you will still be paying 35 to 40 cents on the dollar, or $350,000 to $400,000 in taxes come April 15. If there's no cash and it's just a paper profit, you'll have to borrow $400,000 to pay the IRS. In other words, you are screwed.

You should have been making a profit throughout the year, and a significant piece of that net gain should be sitting in your checking account at all times. If you are truly profitable, you should not have cash flow issues. I don't care how bad the economy gets. If you are watching your bottom line and drying up all the money leaks, you should be able to sleep at night knowing there's always going to be enough money in the bank to give you a nice, soft cushion. The culmination of the whole business cycle must be a tidy pile of cash you can use to pay yourself a reasonable wage and reinvest in the continued success and growth of your business.

In the game of business, pure profits are the only prize.

Profits Are the *Only* Thing

Run your business by the numbers. Profits and cash
are the only true measure of the health of your business.

■

Do a profit and loss statement weekly.

■

Focus on cash flow and expenses NOW. If money is tight,
cut costs viciously. Then cut some more.

■

Collect on those receivables.
Make sure profits on the books translate into cash in the bank.

End Denial

IF IT WEREN'T FOR the four-foot wide conference table between them, Chris Mosca was convinced the retired four-star general was going to snap his neck.

Chris, our senior vice president in charge of corporate surveys, who also happens to be Lou's brother, had been in Texas for six days. He was drilling down into the mess left of a body shop that contracted out staff for government information technology work. The general, a graduate of West Point, owed millions to friends and family. His bank was going to pull all his loans in sixty days. He collateralized his line of credit against his first wife's home and wound up losing it. He couldn't even afford to pay his child support.

This guy had the kind of military record that makes you proud to be an American. But he messed up. It was so bad, he was contemplating suicide, thinking he could pass it off as an accident so his family could use the insurance money to pay off his debts and not be left destitute.

As he spilled all this to Chris, it was clear his life was a pendulum swinging between despair and desperation. But he still had some fight in him and he wasn't quite ready to hand over control to us. He was in such deep denial he couldn't believe that with all his military experience, hard work, and connections he had failed at running his business. At one point he pounded his fist on the table, shouting, *"I will not fail! I will not go bankrupt!"* He stared at Chris in defiance. Then he buried his face in his hands and wept. After a few minutes, when the crying jag was over, Chris stood up, put his hands flat on the table, stared the general straight in the eye, and said, "So are you a coward? What are you gonna do? Walk away?"

That's when the general lost it. He was shaking with blind rage. Chris apologized for being so blunt. But after the general calmed down, and as the veins bulging on his neck subsided, a change came over him. He went quiet. We'd broken him down and made him see the truth. An iron will wasn't going to fix this situation. He couldn't fight this war by himself.

"Even if you charge me $5,000 to help me out of this, I couldn't pay it," he told Chris, sliding the keys to his office across the table. "Take these. The business is yours. I don't know if you can save my company, but I can't."

For the next three months we took over. We put in place airtight controls. We cleaned house and stopped all the money leaks. We got the cash flowing again. The business was viable, it's just that the general had lost control of it. But it didn't take long before he was back in command. Within a year he'd paid back most of his debts, and he was turning a nice, healthy profit. Ten years later he's semi-retired and running operations from his new home in Florida. But before he got there, we had to break him down and make him face the cold hard truth.

That was an extreme case, but we've seen plenty. Small business owners have an extraordinary capacity for deluding themselves until they are broke. A more recent example is a printing company in Lancaster, Pennsylvania. Sales slid from $20 million to $6 million in seven years. The company's line of credit went from zero to $3 million. Its entire net worth, built up over dozens of years, vanished in four. The bank, which was getting ready to cut its credit line, wanted its $4 million in loans repaid, and was giving the business ninety days to find a new lender or it would foreclose. Chapter 11 was right around the corner.

The owner blamed the economy, but the local printing market was thriving. He was losing business to the competition.

The economy is a favorite excuse. But this CEO's business was failing because his only real talent was in sales and he hadn't come out from behind his desk in seven years. He was too busy spending money on yachts, a share in a private plane, and jewelry for his mistresses. He'd handed the reins of the company to his best friend, who'd set up his own business in the back of the shop and was fixing up expensive printing equipment and selling it to the competition, pocketing the proceeds for himself.

Denial Isn't Just a River in Egypt

Denial's rampant in small business. Every time we make a client call, we have to tell them, "Snap out of your coma. Stop pretending you are making money. Stop pretending employees are productive and business is good. It's about facing reality. Business is not doing well, and sales have been down for three years!"

One of the most egregious cases of denial I've ever seen was at a once-successful Harley Davidson dealership in Washington state.

The owner, whom we'll call Harriet the Harley Lady, founded the dealership along with her husband in the 1960s. The business had become a part of the fabric of the community where it was based. It had a clothing and accessory shop, a service and parts department, a gas station and repair shop, and a restaurant. They sold everything from belt buckles and boots to custom and vintage bikes worth about $150,000 each. This little motorbike empire was bringing about $12 million in revenue. But it was only breaking even. They were no longer the only Harley dealership in town, and Harriet needed to make some major adjustments to adapt to the changing marketplace.

But she was a maniac. This eighty-year-old widow lived and breathed the lifestyle. She'd pull up to work everyday on her chopper in her black leather biker garb, with her fifty-year-old boyfriend riding along beside her. She was no sweet little granny who stays home and knits. I don't know if she had tattoos, and I don't want to know, but she probably did. She was a diehard biker chick, and she expected everyone on her staff to devote themselves to the Harley brand. Employees had to participate in the rides and tours, even if there was work to be done. As is the case with many established Harley dealerships, they organized AIDS rides, supported Vietnam vets, and helped political candidates. The business wasn't just about making money, it was about a *culture*, or a counter culture, and that's all Harriet cared about.

But her children—who were in their fifties—were getting concerned. They could see profits weren't what they used to be when their parents first started the business, and they were aware that their matriarch, however feisty, wouldn't be around forever. They wanted to put systems into place that would facilitate a smooth transition to the next generation of ownership. They wanted to establish a profit plan for each department, find out where they were losing the most cash, and tighten up the sales team so they could remain competitive.

A decade ago, an exclusive dealership of any kind was a license to print money, whether it was for GM, Chevrolet, Honda, or Harley. They were almost guaranteed that a certain subset of wealthy, aging baby boomers would be willing to invest high five- and six-figure sums to become weekend HOGs. That is no longer the case. But Harriet believed she would continue to have a loyal and growing customer base. She was wrong.

I sent Chris Mosca to do our survey—a two-to-three week initial review of the strengths, weaknesses, profit leaks, and opportunities for improvement. Chris was the perfect guy to send, because he was a biker back in his younger years and he understood the mindset. Chris won Harriet over. He told her he would select the son or daughter qualified to take over the business and groom them to lead. He zeroed in on the son with an accounting background who seemed to understand what needed to be done and had an appropriate sense of urgency about the need to build profits and keep the cash.

But as soon as we sent our consultants to the site to implement some tough changes, the Harley Queen lost her mind. She fired us five times in three months. There was no rationale behind her objections. She just couldn't accept that the business was in trouble and had to change. She responded by swearing like a truck driver. She overruled every decision that was made not because it wasn't beneficial to her business, but because it wasn't *her* decision.

By the fifth and final time our consultants were fired, the business was actually starting to turn around. The Harley dealership was enjoying real profit growth and cash flow was back on track. The systems of accountability we'd installed were beginning to pay off. But one day, in the middle of the afternoon, Harriet walked into the Harley café kitchen and caught one of her sons with a waitress getting busy by the meat locker. It just so happened that his wife worked on the premises, in the dealership office.

Harriet was furious, and determined for someone to blame besides her own knucklehead son. Us.

"Well, since you guys are supposed to be so omniscient, you should have known about this!" she roared.

It was her excuse to get rid of us. We fought her on it as best we could, but we were no match for a woman whom one of our consultants likened to "Donald Trump on steroids." Now the business is back where it started: losing money.

The tragedy of this story is that Harriet identified herself with her business. She believed they were both immortal. She was an elderly woman whose way of doing business was obsolete, and she refused to see it. By staying on that path, the Harley dealership was more likely to die before she did. After decades of devotion to her business, Harriet and her offspring would likely end up with nothing.

A change in attitude can make the difference between the life and death of a business, which is why we get confrontational. A few prospective clients in denial ask us to leave because they aren't ready to hear the truth. We shake hands and part friends. But the reality is if we're going to get the owners to change, we have to smack them around a bit. It's our job. We have to induce emotional pain to get them to a place where they want to change.

Optimism is all well and good, but I've met business owners who can't even tell me what their bank balance is. They should be coming in each day and asking the tough questions of themselves and everyone who works for them. Once they get to the truth, they need to tackle the unpleasant tasks that need to get done—such as firing people—without delay. Procrastination is denial's best friend, which is why I also tell my clients:

Eat Your Vegetables First!

Remember when you were a kid and sat at the dinner table, shoving peas around the plate with your fork? You ate the meatloaf, the mashed potatoes and the gravy, and put off the green stuff until the end, when it was cold and congealed. You couldn't face eating it, because there was nothing else on the plate to make them more palatable.

That's what business owners do daily. Each of us gets up every morning with several things we don't want to do: meeting with an employee to issue a stern warning about his or her performance; going over last week's expense reports in painstaking detail; calling the bank to find out about renewing a credit line; meeting with department heads to discuss their overall poor performance and ways to improve it; or, calling a major customer you fear is about to dump your company as a vendor. It's much more pleasant to head for that business lunch or mid-afternoon golf tournament, telling yourself it's an important opportunity to network. But that would be a mistake.

If there's a difficult task on your "to do" list that you've been putting off, do it first and do it now. Are three out of ten employees failing miserably? Fire them! Is your biggest problem that you need a new banking institution? Don't waste time shooting the breeze with clients. Make the calls and find the bank with the best loan terms. Suck it up and do it!

The longer these tasks don't get done, the more problems will accumulate. Putting off the stuff you don't want to do is just another sign you are in denial. Tackle it head-on and get it over with. Eat your vegetables.

Look for the Red Flags

Because if you don't, soon all you'll be seeing is red ink. The signs will be obvious enough if you're looking for them. If you're living week to week to cover operational costs; if your line of credit is maxing out; if your knuckles turn white every time you try to meet payroll; if all you see at 5 p.m. on Friday or Saturday morning is an empty parking lot outside, you'll know you've got some serious problems.

Facing up to reality is never easy. As we did with the general and the owner of the print shop, we put each new client through a corporate survey that assesses the client's strengths and weaknesses as a business. This survey also helps break the denial habit. We're hired to tell business owners what's wrong, not how good they are. When we ask them how they think their business is doing, we get a list of excuses and justifications for why its failing: "Oh, I'm going through a divorce. It's the economy. My sales team isn't performing the way it should be. I'm going to get a new bank loan. We're starting a new ad campaign next month, yeah, that should turn things around." They're in fantasy land.

We force them to do a self-appraisal in the cold light of day. Then we ask their employees—managers and workers—how *they* think the business is doing. We don't reveal any names, and we don't get personal—we keep it honest. Usually, five out of six managers will say things aren't changing for the better and morale is not good. The owner's wife, who does the bookkeeping, is incompetent. His three kids in sales are useless. The list goes on, and the answers are almost always contrary to what the owner thinks.

At that point in the process, it gets heavy. People run out of the room. Our analysts have to duck and cover. There are tears, screaming matches, threats of divorce, and sometimes fistfights. Some people quit right on the spot. This is good. It's a start. Because you can't fix things until you know what's wrong. We don't care about your ego or the feelings of the people on your payroll.

Taking a cold hard look at yourself and your business can be the toughest thing for an owner to do. But the truth test is necessary. You have to understand where the leaks are in the business, and exactly how, as the boss, it's your fault. You have to wake up before you can make more profits. Denial is the small business owner's worst enemy. End it now. Face whatever it takes to build a stronger business.

Are you in denial? Have bad habits like procrastination and self-indulgence bled your profits dry? It's time to assess your leadership. Answer the following questions as honestly as possible. Don't worry. No one's reading over your shoulder. The only person who has to handle the truth is you.

Denial Pop Quiz

You give someone a task that must be completed as soon as possible. How long do you wait before checking in on him?

A: 2 days

B: 1 day

C: 'Til the end of the day

D: You mean it isn't done yet?

Describe how your employees view you:

A: The nicest boss ever

B: Tough but fair

C: Demanding and stern

D: Genghis Khan would be easier to work for, but our profits are through the roof!

You hired a friend who just isn't cutting the mustard. How do you address it?

A: Give her a little more time and see if her work improves

B: Sit him down and try to motivate him

C: Explain to her she needs to step up

D: Tell him you heard Burger King is hiring and "Good luck!"

Your cash situation is:

A: No idea. You're too busy maxing out your line of credit.

B: Tight right now, but you'll make it up with better sales next month.

C: Profits look great on paper, if only your clients would pay what they owe you on time.

D: Cash flow is so good you're wondering how best to invest the money.

How many excuses do you hear a day?

A: 3 to 4, but they're usually legitimate

B: More than you care to hear

C: You're going to belt the next guy who gives one.

D: None. Excuses are meaningless. You just want to hear that the job is done.

How closely do you monitor each department?

A: Weekly

B: Daily

C: Hourly

D: You didn't read the question because you're doing it right now.

A game of golf is:

A: A great way to make business deals and network

B: A good way to suck up to your bank manager when necessary

C: A fine way to relax, but only after hours

D: A colossal waste of time

If your business isn't turning a profit, who's to blame?

A: The sales staff

B: The sales manager

C: The faltering economy

D: Take a look in the mirror and make a few guesses

What do you consider to be the most accurate barometer of your businesses success?

A: Profits and cash

B: Profits and cash

C: Profits and cash

D: Profits and cash

If you answered:

Mostly A's and B's: You have no business owning a business. How are you at pumping gas?

Mostly C's: There may be hope for you yet, but you're probably just scraping by. Time for some serious changes.

Mostly D's: You're on the right track, but there's always more you can do to maximize profits. Read on to find out how.

End Denial

Snap out of your coma today. Open the books, look at where you are
financially and face reality: profits are not what they should be.

■

Look for red flags.

■

Eat your vegetables first. Procrastination is denial's best friend.
If there's someone you need to fire, deal with it!

■

Take the truth test: Ask yourself honestly where you think the
business is doing well, and where you need major surgery.

■

Ask your managers to do the same, anonymously.
You might be surprised by their answers.

Forget Sweat Equity

An alarming number of business owners believe that when they're building a business they shouldn't pay themselves a salary. They sacrifice their own income for many years to get their business up and running. Venture capitalists call this "sweat equity." I call it working for nothing and being a fool.

When I see owners not paying themselves the full value of their services, I shudder. The inability to pay yourself a reasonable salary is a red flag that your business is not working. Making loans to the company so you can pay yourself, and not charging the company rent if you own the building, are equally foolish. Ask yourself this question: If your business doesn't allow you to pay yourself a living wage, what are you doing wrong?

Of the more than 6,000 small businesses we've worked with, I can't think of a single one that failed because the owner paid himself or herself a decent salary. You've got to take care of yourself first. You are the one who holds all the risk, so you should reap the rewards. Not only is it looking out for Number One to pay yourself a reasonable income, it's taking care of business.

You Can't Lead the Way If You're Behind the Pack

You'd be amazed at how many of our clients and experts fight us on this one. You may think that sacrificing yourself is the right thing to do, because if cuts have to be made and money saved, you should take the hit and lead by example. But cutting costs doesn't mean you should make yourself the company's sacrificial lamb. Take a 5 percent cut along with the rest of your staff, but don't put a 30 percent pay cut on your own back. In tough times everyone should make adjustments. There are some short periods when you might have to sacrifice your income, but doing so is symptomatic of a much deeper financial problem.

Owners always tell us they fear employees will leave if they cut payroll. Good! If they're that uncommitted to the job, why would you want them to stick around? Trust me, lousy workers are expendable (more on this later). You can always hire someone better for less. You are not in business to be a benefactor. You started your company to make money and build wealth. Why work for free so others don't have to tighten their belts?

Why are you putting employees' pockets first when you've collateralized your home for a $1 million line of credit? At least 70 percent of our business owners have a line of credit on their business that's almost tapped out. They have to sign personal guarantees. Their husbands or wives have to sign too. They can't collateralize these loans with their business, so they do it with their houses and retirement funds. It is the business owner, and the business owner alone, who puts home and future at risk. If you have one hundred employees, I guarantee they won't be writing you a check for $10,000 each to back up the business.

The term *sweat equity* applies more appropriately to venture capital situations with outside investors who put millions at risk on your plan. In these situations, paying yourself less than your market value is okay for a while, but don't make it a cause celeb. In most cases, the venture capitalists demand much, but they aren't investing their own money.

Instead of investing sweat equity, focus on fixing your business model. It doesn't matter if you own a restaurant, a construction company, or a limo service. Lack of sales or quality controls, bloated overhead, and other financial woes are the real reasons you're not taking a salary. Shame on you, not your employees, for failing to make sufficient profits.

Many of our clients own the premises their business operates from outright and don't charge the business rent. It's just another way of masking poor performance. It's another form of denial that's going to lead to failure. If your business is barely breaking even, why not just shut the business down tomorrow, rent out the building, and pay yourself $300,000 a year? It's better than breaking your back for no return.

There Are No Rich Martyrs

Most business owners underpay themselves. There's a pervasive belief among small business owners that "One day I'll get mine." These are good people raised with the simple edict that you should work hard, treat people fairly, and be patient. When they have a bad year with no profits, they take a second mortgage on their homes so they can afford to pay their workers a holiday bonus. It's nice to treat people fairly, but not at your expense.

They think if they keep sacrificing they'll eventually be able to sell the business and retire. But the sad fact is that there's often nothing left to sell when the time comes. This mindset doesn't get them a condo in Florida and a comfortable nest egg. It gets them nothing but a large amount of personal debt. Instead of accumulating wealth, they've slaved at a job for decades just to cover payroll and pay the bills.

Always work to make a good salary. Then cover the expenses. Not the other way around. If the numbers don't line up, don't even start, because you'll always be fighting an uphill battle to stay ahead of your expenses. This a basic issue of survival. How are you going to make that climb if you are not setting aside enough cash for your own well-being?

And the Loser Is . . .

We did a client survey in Maryland recently with the owner of a $14 million company that manufactures trophies. Bill, the second-generation owner, was the nicest guy you could ever meet. He'd cut his pay from $150,000 to $100,000 over the last year in an effort to cut expenses and put more money back into the company. This guy cared about his business. With profits down and the line of credit tapped out, cutting his salary was his way of solving the problem.

We told him to give himself a substantial raise, but he balked. Bill kept insisting he was responsible so he was the one who had to take a hit. We hammered away at him and finally, ten days into the job, he took me aside.

"George, can I level with you? I need to talk with you alone."

"Sure, Bill," I said. "Let's take a walk."

It was a cold and rainy December day, but we took a long stroll around the block, making sure we were out of earshot from any employees.

"You've finally made me realize something," Bill said. "All these years, I've been running on fumes. My entire adult life has been consumed by this business, and through it all I've never really gotten what I wanted. I've worked for my family, I've slaved and sacrificed for my employees, but I've never really done anything for myself."

"Well," I said, "when are you going to start?"

"Right now!" Bill said. "All that self-sacrifice did nothing but hold me back. I am taking your advice and giving myself a raise."

Bill had lost sight of why he was running a business in the first place—to make his life better. He doubled his salary and, as soon as he did, he took a new approach to running the business. He had more energy and it showed. His employees and family members saw a dynamic business leader instead of a poor schmuck. Within a year, profits saw double digit improvements. Our job was done.

The desire to create wealth and live a comfortable existence isn't a crime. It's what we're here for. It's the whole point. It's what motivates us to make a profit and build a viable business that puts cash into our pockets both now and in the future. Sure, take care of your employees. Reward and motivate the best workers. But the ownership has to come first. Sacrifice and commitment only get you so far. You also need to be selfish.

Because You're Worth It

Don't be a pin cushion so everyone else will be okay. Ask yourself how much you'd pay a general manager to run your business if you had to go away. That's the least you should be paying yourself to run things.

I started my own business more than twenty years ago with $42,000. I saw what I believed was a great opportunity to work with underserved small and midsized businesses. The numbers looked as if I could make a great living and build an enduring place in the market for American Management Services. I care about building success for our clients, but have no interest in working for peanuts. I have always worked hard to maximize profits for my company. Our commitment to profitability has allowed us to grow and prosper.

Along the way I've been fortunate enough to have accumulated waterfront homes in Palm Beach and Nantucket. I indulge in one of my greatest passions, philanthropy, contributing millions of dollars to dozens of charitable foundations. I live well off the fruits of my hard work. I built our business to get rich, not to become a martyr to it, and you shouldn't become one to your business either. Be careful not to overdo displays of conspicuous consumption, but by all means enjoy the good life. You deserve it.

Once in a while we come across a client who has no problem with this principle. We had a paving contractor client in Florida a year ago whose annual revenue was $10 million, out of which he put $1.5 million in his pocket. This guy was no chump. He never lost sight of the fact he was in business to enrich himself, and if he can do that and continue to sustain the business, more power to him.

Of course, 15 percent of revenue was a little high. A lot of small businesses don't have profit margins that size. Shortsighted greed can kill a business. It was too late for us to save a car dealership that went out of business by the time we got the call. It might have stood a chance if Dad hadn't been taking all the money out of the business to build himself a house in the Poconos. He left his son and son-in-law on the hook for a loan collateralized with their own homes, which they lost.

Reward yourself, but within reason. We have established a rough formula for how much salary business owners should pay themselves, before profit distributions. Pay yourself 3 to 4 cents on each dollar of revenue for doing the job of CEO. If you have a $10 million business, the ownership, whether it is a sole proprietorship or there are partners, should be receiving $300,000 to $400,000 in total salary. Remember, after you and the owners pay yourselves salaries, your business should still be making profits equal to the top quarter of your industry, not the bottom half.

Sweat Shop Equity

We recently worked with an Asian family-owned garment business in Miami that took sweat equity to a whole new level. The company, which had annual sales of $8 million, imported suits for small chain retailers. The mother, let's call her "Mrs. Chan," was the majority shareholder, but she paid herself only $32,000 a year. She was working six days a week, and long hours, for a lousy $4.80 an hour.

When I asked her why she was working for less than minimum wage, Mrs. Chan explained to me that she owned the building and rather than take her income out of the business, she took rent from the premises. Rent was $150,000 a year. I asked her how much property taxes and maintenance cost. About $50,000, she said. That meant her take home was about $125,000. But fair market value to rent the building would have been about $300,000. Mrs. Chan was trying to do the honorable thing and sacrifice her own needs for her employees and her family, but she was fooling herself. Everyone else was fine, but she'd imposed sweatshop conditions on herself. She was not giving herself a fair wage, and she wasn't taking what she was entitled to as the owner.

This muddled math caused her to overlook some critical details about her business. She missed that her company was leaking $580,000 in profits. The pricing, costing, and purchasing processes were all wrong. Inventory and cash management were a disaster. Mrs. Chan thought they were doing pretty well collecting money, but they weren't getting paid for seventy-five days when she thought it was sixty days. By underpaying herself she was unintentionally hiding major pricing flaws and other rampant failures in her operations. She was probably so tired from being overworked and underpaid that she couldn't lift her head off the table to see what was going on. She was in serious trouble.

But when we put the real numbers down for Mrs. Chan in black and white, it didn't take much begging and cajoling to get her to pay herself properly. She gave herself a raise, changed her pricing system, cleaned up inventory, plugged the cash leaks, and closed the gaps on her long list of receivables. A year later, profits were up 35 percent.

Pipe Dreams up in Smoke

Sweat equity doesn't only mask problems in the business. It sends a message to employees that weakens your position as leader. A few years ago we worked with a pipe distributor in central New Jersey struggling with lousy morale. With $17 million in revenues the company was marginally profitable, but management was so dysfunctional it was eroding the bottom line.

The founder and owner of the company, Joe, who was sixty-five, worked tirelessly and never transferred equity to his three sons. He didn't really trust them. But out of guilt, or some misplaced sense of filial duty, he gave them exalted titles and paid them $130,000 each. He was only paying himself $90,000.

This compromise opened the door to disaster. The three sons, who were in their forties, had fistfights and screaming matches over who was in charge. (More on family dysfunction in Chapter 5.) One son quit in the middle of an important client transaction when he found out he was not the chosen heir to the business. The other two, each of whom handled some aspect of sales, camped out in offices on opposite sides of the building, while their father shut himself inside his own office to avoid the family strife.

The tension was palpable. We realized, after two days on-site, that the employees had no idea who to look to for leadership. Each brother thought the company was his, and that they were entitled to fat salaries and ownership because they brought in the biggest haul of sales. But one of the sons waltzed in late every morning because he liked to get in a long workout at the gym before starting his day. The other son disappeared for long lunches and knocked off early, purportedly to schmooze clients. Still, the numbers told a different story about their contributions to the business. Neither was particularly effective at sales.

Employees kept their heads down. The office floor didn't have the usual hum of chit chat, just the occasional outburst of anger between the two brothers. Internal politics were rife, as employees had to choose sides and report to one brother or the other, but never both. Father and sons each thought they were in charge, but no one had control. Joe had to spend all his energy being mediator and peacemaker between his squabbling children.

Our first step was to give the patriarch a fat raise. We changed Joe's salary up to $250,000. He protested, but we told him:

"Do you want to be viewed as the boss and get control back, or don't you?"

Salary has a huge impact on how your employees perceive you. The big boss has to get the big bucks. The spoils must go to the alpha dog. It's simple human psychology. If you reward yourself less than your employees, be they family members or civilians, you undermine your credibility. You send the message that you somehow see yourself as worth less than others, and that is how you will be treated. And don't kid yourself into thinking your salary is confidential. Everybody knows.

Paying Dad double sent a clear message. We had to make sure it was understood that Joe was in charge until he chose not to be. But we weren't done yet. We cut his sons down to size and demoted them from sales managers to sales reps. They weren't paid less, but they were put in their place.

Even though we added an extra $160,000 to payroll by raising the father's salary, profits improved substantially after that change. Employee morale got a big boost and the sons got the message that they had to earn their keep. We implemented pay for performance, so they'd get paid more if they made good sales (more on this later). We also let it be known they were years away from taking control of the company. Nothing could be taken for granted.

Frank the Plumber

Soon after we worked with the pipe distributor, we got a call from another small business, a plumbing contractor in Idaho. Again, it was a second-generation, multimillion-dollar business. But it wasn't the sons who were taking home a disproportionately high paycheck. It was the patriarch. We'll call him "Uncle Frank."

Uncle Frank was not the owner. Far from it. The sons held most of the equity in the business they'd inherited from their father, who had passed away several years ago. Uncle Frank, who held a paltry 4 percent stake, then took on Dad's role, giving the two boys guidance while they were still green and unfamiliar with the ins and outs of the business.

But as the two sons matured, they took over responsibility for the company. They were running it just fine except for one thing: They were paying themselves next to nothing with a combined salary of $150,000 and remunerating Uncle Frank to the tune of $350,000. In other words, the next generation of business owners was fighting for their personal survival on pennies to a dollar, and killing themselves to keep their business going. They were in their late forties and they had nothing to show for it.

Uncle Frank didn't care. It wasn't his neck. He didn't have to collateralize his assets to guarantee bank loans. All he did was pop his head into the office to interfere for one or two hours a day, then go off home to take an afternoon nap or play a few rounds of golf. He was a freeloader. His fat salary became an entitlement, and it was becoming a major strain on payroll. Other expenses that could have benefited the business had to be sacrificed to pay Uncle Frank, and their cousin, Uncle Frank's deadbeat son, Frankie Junior, who was getting paid $70,000 a year to do nothing. A total of $430,000 a year was going out the door because the de facto patriarch insisted it had to be that way.

The two sons were exhausted. Business had been going well, but recent ups and downs in the construction industry meant the company was barely breaking even. Employees were confused as to whether they were working for the uncle or the nephews. Bad decisions were being made because the actual owners, Uncle Frank's nephews, were not taking care of themselves.

It took us three months to convince Uncle Frank it was time to take a pay cut. There's a birth order in these family run businesses that's almost impossible to break. The brothers were afraid to confront their uncle, because he'd been like a father to them over the years—or so it seemed—and nobody tells the dad what to do. Uncle Frank was 5'4", but they were terrified of him. The diminutive old man considered himself to be the owner of the company, regardless of how little stock he had, and the two sons, who were majority stakeholders, allowed themselves to be treated like employees. Instead of being the true heirs of their father's business, they were acting like the poor cousins whose job it was to enrich the surviving patriarch.

We had to force a change in thinking. We had to meet with Uncle Frank's financial advisor and show him in black and white how his excessive salary was to the detriment of the business. Finally, we convinced him that if Uncle Frank kept taking his oversized paycheck, he would jeopardize the future of the business. There would soon be nothing left for anyone. The financial advisor got the message, and conveyed it to Uncle Frank, who grudgingly agreed to a 50 percent pay cut and allowed us to fire Frankie Junior.

We also more than doubled the salaries of the two brothers running the show. Today business is slowly improving despite the steep downturn in the construction business. The changes we made gave the true owners a shot in the arm, and that renewed energy is translating into better sales and smarter management decisions.

Paying yourself is not just a way of keeping check on the health of the business. If you're sacrificing yourself and scaling back on expenses for yourself and your family, you're not in the best position to lead. You have to take care of yourself first so you can stay sharp and become the kind of boss you need to be to take your business to the next level. You have a duty to your business, your family, and your employees. Most of all, you have a duty to yourself. You're the one who signs the checks on the front, takes all the risks, and lies awake at night, so you should be the first to sign the check on the back.

Forget Sweat Equity

For small business owners, what venture capitalists call "sweat equity"
is no more than working for nothing and being a fool.

■

Take care of yourself first and the rest will follow.
You can't lead the way if you're behind the pack.

■

If things are tight, don't be the only one to take a pay cut.
You're not in business to be everyone else's benefactor.

■

If you can't afford to pay yourself the first few cents on every dollar,
there's something seriously wrong with your business model. Fix it!

■

Money talks. Show who's the boss by paying yourself like one.

■

Remember, there are no rich martyrs.

Love Your Business More Than Your Family

CENTURIES AGO, WHEN I went to Harvard Business School, I took a course on entrepreneurship that was the only one of its kind at the time (there are about a dozen today). The class was popular. The professor was a brilliant contrarian whose ideas have guided the creation of hundreds of successful and innovative businesses. He said something that first day of class that has stayed with me ever since.

He asked us, "Will all the married students please stand up?"

About half the class got out of their seats (not me), and the professor asked them to leave. He told them that a family would get in the way of their success, so there wasn't much point in them taking his course. Everyone was confused and murmuring to each other. Visibly upset, one of the married students stood up to ask, "Why?"

"Go back to your seats; you can stay in the class," the professor said. "But I wasn't kidding."

That was in the early 1970s, long before anyone had heard the word *Internet*. There were no personal computers, let alone Blackberries, cell phones, or voice mail. To run your business, you had to be there all hours. It was a full-time commitment. Today, with the ability to maintain constant contact, the bar has been raised and there is even less excuse not to be in touch and on top of your business 24/7. Wherever you are, you have dozens of options for getting the work done and checking in. So do it.

Business First

I think of what this professor said every time I meet clients who fail to be fully committed to the success of their business. Cutting out early to take your kids to baseball practice three times a week, printing up invitations for your church fundraiser, or picking up your Aunt Tilly or Uncle Ned from the airport—these are all unacceptable interruptions to success. Your cell phone is for keeping in touch with clients and sales managers in the field, NOT for taking calls from your spouse throughout the day about what groceries to pick up on the way home. You can keep doing these things and waste dozens of hours each week. Or you can focus on the financial future of business and work all day, every day, including Saturdays and Sundays!

If you're not focused—if family, friends, community and church fill up your busy weekly schedule—you are probably failing to deliver real profits for your company.

When I do seminars around the country about building profits, it always stuns me when more than half the people in the room admit to not working on weekends, yet these are the same people who complain about failing to make big money. They tell me they sometimes work from home but, when pushed, admit they are doing it half-heartedly, with a football game on television or while cooking the family dinner. If you can't be focused while working from home, don't bother.

I meet a lot of resistance to this from clients at first. They get angry. They say, "So what if I want to put my family first?" "Don't you dare tell me not to go to church!" "I deserve a normal life!"

Sure you do. Of course you have every right to a life—if you don't care about making money. Go to that ball game. A smart person, Bill Collier, wrote a bestselling book, *How to Succeed as a Small Business Owner . . . and Still Have a Life*. It all sounds great on paper, but it's never going to happen. The easy money has dried up. You can't make a profit anymore just by selling a slimmer cell phone or a tastier energy drink. But you have your priorities, and I understand. If you don't want to put your business before all other considerations, by all means sell up or prepare yourself for a life of financial mediocrity.

This *Is* for Your Family

The husband or wife might squawk when you shut off your cell phone during meetings and tell them only to call for an emergency. Johnny and Suzy might stamp their feet or pout when you don't make it to the baseball game or the ballet recital. But here's a news flash: They'd much rather enjoy great financial security than see you struggling for the rest of your life to make money that never comes.

You are the only person who is going to fix your business and make it better, and that is not going to happen while you are taking fourteen personal phone calls a day and attending local cub scout meetings three times a week.

We worked with a family-owned specialty biscuit company in

Memphis a few years back in serious financial trouble. As far as I was concerned the fault lay with one of the partners, the sister, who was in charge of purchasing. She always put business last.

The company's main sources for product were all in Mexico, but Sis refused to travel. She claimed her commitment to her kids prevented her from taking even two weeks out of her schedule to go there. She regularly took the equivalent of a couple of days off a week for parent-teacher meetings and other personal commitments, even though she expected a full-time paycheck.

We convinced her siblings to buy her out and replace her with a professional purchasing agent willing to work sixty hours a week and go to the far ends of the globe in the search for competitively priced quality product. As a direct result, the company saved $2 million a year.

That's how much the sister/co-owner's lack of commitment cost the business. And yet this woman was the first to complain to her brothers and sisters that she wasn't making enough money to cover hefty personal expenses and couldn't afford to send her kids off to a good college.

We spend a lot of our time explaining to ownership that their business is not a part-time job. This summer we worked with a landscaper in Minnesota wallowing in financial mediocrity. Sales were down by 50 percent, and it was clear that bankruptcy wasn't far off. But the owner was more interested in the weather forecast than his profit outlook. On every nice day of the week he was out on the lake with his power boat. To him, being out there on the water was more sacred than making money and nothing we could do would make him see the light. Time will tell, but when we checked in with him recently it looked as though his business was well on the way to failure.

Worthier pursuits are just as fatal to the profitability of your business.

In my cross-country seminars, we have a session on time conflicts, and the business owners in the audience who seem to care the most about being community leaders make the least amount of money every month. They act more like they are running a nonprofit than a business. They are barely subsisting financially, yet they are the ones getting involved in local politics, the boy scouts, church, and charity boards. They are the first to fail.

Four years ago we worked with a food manufacturer in Oklahoma actively involved in community work. When we showed up, he cut our first meeting short because he had an appointment with the governor. The next day he had to meet with the mayor. He attended political rallies at least three times a week and became a prominent member of his community, and it was all because he cared about the people of his town and state. The problem was his $17 million manufacturing business was bleeding cash. The owner could barely pay his country club dues.

We worked with him for the next year. We explained that he was running a multimillion-dollar enterprise, not a political campaign. We told him he had to cut back on his financial and time commitments to local politics or face certain death in his business. Did he believe he'd keep getting invited to luncheons with the governor if he had no money left to write him those checks?

He heard us. As a business person, he'd lost his center. When he took a hard look at his financials, he soon found himself again. He got back to work and within two years he was making more than $1 million a year in profits. His profit margin surpassed 7 percent, putting him in the top quartile of his industry. And it was all because he shifted his priorities back to the financial well-being of his first love: his business.

Saturdays and Sundays Are for Work!

The commitment it takes to reach that level of profitability in your business does not stop at 5 o'clock on Friday. I know you probably think you are entitled to spend the weekend recharging, catching up with family, or worshipping God. But I don't care, and neither does your business. Weekends are for work.

Sure, you should probably go to your church, or temple, or mosque, and pray for profits—because many times you will need divine intervention to overcome your lousy decisions and foolish ways. But the second you get up off your knees, head straight back to the office, because this profit rule applies to everything that takes time away from your business, however sacred.

Don't get me wrong. I have the utmost respect for the millions of God-fearing business owners across America. I've prayed with them and I've prayed for them. Absolutely go to church on Sunday or temple on Saturday. Religion is a worthy pursuit. But what are you doing for the rest of the day? That hour or two you've spent meditating or worshipping may be just the thing you need to clear your head and get you ready to tackle the bookkeeping and sales reports for the rest of the afternoon.

If you want your small business to excel, you've only got seven days a week to make it happen. Use that time wisely. Remember, while your competitors are at the BBQ, fishing up at the lake, or attending their kids' softball games, you are putting in the hours necessary to build the business and make profits. When you started your business, that's what you signed on for. Don't fall off the path now. When your company starts flourishing and operations are running smoothly, you'll have even more reason to praise God or spend quality time with your family.

Be There or Be Broke

If you own a business and you're not happy with what's going on inside its four walls, the solution is simple: *show up!*

We had a client—a pool installation business in New Mexico—where the eight family members running it kept wildly erratic hours. The CFO kept leaving at 4 o'clock to pick her kids up from soccer, claiming she'd work from home for the rest of the day. Her brother, meanwhile, the only single sibling in the clan, put in the most hours and sold the most pools. He made side deals with local landscapers and contractors, and kept the kickbacks for himself. When we asked him why he felt it was okay to steal from the family, he said:

"How the hell do you think I am skimming? We all get paid the same salary, but my sister works a twenty-five-hour week and I work sixty hours! Who is stealing from whom?" It's no way to run a business, but the guy had a point.

Pray for Profits

We always ask our clients how hard they are willing to work, and how often they come in on Saturdays and Sundays. Too often the answer is not enough, and almost never on Sundays.

You've got to love your business more than anything. We had a client in Maryland—a father, son, and son-in-law team who built homes. All three of them were church ministers. They worked in church on Saturday, held services as ministers on Sunday, and prayed every day at work for at least one hour.

I'm not knocking their faith. These were sincere, good people. But as business owners they were failures, and in the estimation of Chris, whom you met in Chapter 2, they were hiding behind the church. They deluded themselves into thinking they were successful because they always did the "right thing." They never pushed for change orders. They were lenient with workers because they wanted to be kind Christians.

We gave them some tough love. Chris asked the father, "In the eyes of your maker, are you a good shepherd? It seems you are using God as an excuse for being a failure."

Chris made sure he asked for permission to be confrontational before hitting the client with a question like that. The client agreed, but it was obvious the guy wanted to smack himself for allowing it. The next morning he came to Chris and said, "I prayed on it last night, and you're right. I've accepted mediocrity. I want to change."

The three men are still involved in the church, but they're also born-again businessmen. They've put tough controls in place, and they're in the office every day watching the shop, not reading passages from the Bible. They found the balance between faith and financial discipline.

Always on Sundays

The same goes for family. You are going to feel tremendous pressure to attend your child's ballgame or go for a long, country stroll with your husband or wife. Maybe you had a fight on Wednesday, and promised to spend the weekend together and make nice. I don't care. That's what jewelry is for. That's when you treat everybody to a steak dinner. It takes less time, so you can make peace and get on with running your business.

Get your behind to the office. That's where you need to be. Your family will still be there when you get home. Weekends are the perfect time to get work done. The phone's not ringing. There are no distractions. People aren't wandering past your office. The emails aren't overloading your in-box. It can be your most productive time of the week, particularly for backend housekeeping and financials. Hell, have your accountant come in and go over the books with you. Buy her coffee. If she says she can't make it, find another bookkeeper!

When you're retired, wealthy, and able to spend time raising funds for the poorest members of your congregation; when you've built a new parochial school for the children of Botswana; when you have the operational, fingertip controls in place so that you can spend the majority of your time with your kids and grandkids at your winter home in Hilton Head, you'll be glad you gave up a few Sunday afternoons to work your butt off. You'll be pleased that you devoted more time to that other religion: profits.

Love Your Business More Than Your Family

The same goes for church, charity, and other worthy pursuits.

■

Your business is not a part-time job.
Be fully committed and ready to put in the hours.

■

Cutting out early for little Suzy's ballet recital won't cut it.
She'll pout and stamp her feet now, but she'll thank
you later when you can pay for college.

■

Don't work from home unless you can be fully focused.

■

Weekends are for work. Feel free to go to church,
mosque, or temple; then get your behind straight
back to the office. Better yet, pray at your desk.

■

Be there, or be broke.

The Best Family Business Has *One* Member

I HAD A CLIENT in Kentucky—an office supply distributor—who built up his business from nothing into a $16 million-a-year enterprise. His three sons, all in their fifties, were vying with each other to become the chosen heir and run daddy's business when he retired. Two of these grown men ended up in a fistfight in the hallway, right in front of our consultant and the office's horrified staff. Plants were kicked over, pictures were knocked down. People had to duck and jump out of the way.

The third son, who was more responsible and capable than the other two and the obvious choice for taking over the business, left in disgust. He moved out of state to be as far away from the family as possible. The father wound up selling the business so he wouldn't have to pick sides.

Blood and Business Don't Mix

You should see the looks of horror on people's faces when I recount this story in my business seminars. It's always the same. At first, people gasp, and a few even yelp. Then the audience breaks out into a collective giggle. Some are laughing because they are embarrassed. The person sitting right next to them is that sibling, spouse, or in-law who they know isn't pulling their weight. Suddenly, the lecture hall feels uncomfortably claustrophobic. A few awkward moments later I can see the looks of relief on the faces of the business owners, because they've received confirmation that they're not alone with their doubts and suspicions. They're glad someone *else* finally said it. And they know it's true.

Of course there are exceptions. There are ALWAYS exceptions, and you may well be one of them. But read on, because even if you're running a family business that is doing okay, you know profits could be much better without the extra expense of keeping a child, sibling, or in-law on the payroll. If you're really being honest with yourself, you'll recognize many of the dramas described here. And you'll know what to do the next time you bump up against an intractable relative.

Between 60 percent and 70 percent of small businesses are family-owned, and that's where most of their problems start—with the rest of the family. I don't want your kids to hate you. I don't want your husband or wife to storm out of the room. But in my experience with thousands of small businesses, I have found that putting a relative in a role they are not suited for will lead to failure, and it's done way too often.

One of our clients in Charleston, South Carolina created from scratch a chain of four successful (or so I thought) fashionable clothing stores. We had worked with her a decade ago and established strong profitability. I ran into this competent woman recently at a social event and asked her how the business was going.

"It's awful," she replied. "I just had to close one of my stores."

That store had been failing for two years. It was managed by her son. In this tight economy the losses from that store were threatening the company's survival. She began to complain that her son was lazy, never took direction, had a lousy work ethic, and was clueless about business. When I asked her why she hadn't shut the store earlier or replaced the son, she said, "He needs a good job so he can pay all his bills."

So now, after closing the store, she's going to pay him enough money, a few thousand dollars a month, so he can continue his life of luxury. The kicker: The son is forty-three years old! Apparently, he doesn't have any career training except in "filmmaking." Amazingly, she's willing to float him at his advanced age. When I suggested that she cut him off so he could focus on making a living and not continue to indulge his childish whims, she admitted that she just couldn't do it. But she's not doing her son any favors. He needs a firm kick in the pants and out the door.

Cancel Your Kid's Membership to the Lucky Sperm Club

I can appreciate that you really want to write "Smith & Sons (or Daughters)" on your shingle. We all want to be proud of our kids. But hey, if it's not working, it's not working. If you want to leave a legacy, don't allow it to be a pile of unpaid debts. Don't let Tommy or Cindy mismanage the business, get overpaid, and run the company into the ground.

Most problems in family businesses are caused by the incompetence of family members. There's never enough money to go around because the owner is paying people who shouldn't be there, and in small companies there simply isn't that kind of room for failure.

Ninety percent of the time you are giving a position to a family member who is not the best qualified person for the job. If you are looking for a good sales manager, picking a family member in need of a paycheck is insanity. Normally you would advertise for a top candidate out of a pool of dozens with sales and industry experience, a proven record of success, and a strong desire to do the job. Picking from a pool of one or two blood relatives to fill this make-or-break role in the business is, as Spock would say, illogical.

You don't want to put your son-in-law or niece in charge of production because: A) They don't really want to do it, whatever they tell you; B) They probably have no clue; or, C) They've been doing it for ten years and they STILL have no clue. Why take a chance on a family member without the experience and dedication? You are taking a huge risk.

Don't Force a Square Peg into a Round Hole

If your wife would rather go back to law school, your husband prefers to be a stockbroker, or your son wants to go to the Fashion Institute of Technology to become a clothing designer, don't put them in charge of sales. Don't let them do the books. Let them do their thing! They might resent you at first, but in all fairness, they can go off and do something else. You are not going to lose more than you would by having them there. Ultimately, they will be happier, and so will you.

I can hear you asking, "But who else can I trust but my family?" More often than not, that kind of mentality will send you straight into a financial hole you may never climb out of. When it comes to your business, trust no one! Believing that your relatives feel they have as much at stake in the business as you is a fallacy.

Yes, there are some gifted members of the lucky sperm club. In some rare cases, a business can thrive under the second and third generations of family, and relatives don't hurt the bottom line. The son of Bob Kraft, owner of the New England Patriots, has done well for his family's business. It wouldn't be as valuable as it is now without his services. But a successful business heir like Jonathan Kraft is an anomaly.

The story of a successful seafood restaurant chain in the mid-Atlantic illustrates what can happen when you take family foibles out of the equation. This chain, with a father, a few sons, and other family members, had grown to multi-millions in revenue, but hadn't made a serious profit for many years. When the father passed away, the two sons duked it out in court over control of the business. One son and his family members left, leaving just one family member in control. The chain has since multiplied in size and now makes a huge profit. No surprise here.

Car dealers love to pass the baton to their sons and daughters. But it's a low margin business to start with, and the almost certain damage relatives can cause running the shop could sink profits beyond repair. I can't tell you how many mothers and fathers in their mid-fifties I've met who haven't saved a dime for retirement because it's all being spent on the family payroll.

Keep the Family Squabbles at Home

Meanwhile, as blood bleeds your profits dry, the day-to-day operations of the business are in a state of total dysfunction. I've sat in on staff meetings where family members are talking about picking Timmy up from preschool, or demanding an extra two weeks off to go to Disneyland.

I've seen CEOs shrink behind their desks when wives come into the office crying or in a rage because they think Junior, who isn't doing anything for the business, is being mistreated. Family squabbles play out all the time in front of staff, who are left wondering what kind of protection and advancement opportunities they could possibly have within an organization run this way. Allowing home life and all its messy dramas to take over the building is atrocious business practice. But opening the office door to family invites these problems, and worse.

Our company doesn't publicly present itself as a family counseling service, but a good deal of the time that's exactly what we do. I can recall heading to the parking lot at the end of a grueling session with a husband and wife team. It was our job to clean up the financial system of their technology business, which was hemorrhaging cash. The husband followed me to the car, threw his arms around me, and said, "You can't leave me." I didn't know what to do. Neither did the husband. He didn't know where else to turn. Because the problems that are rife in most family businesses are not just about profits and losses. They're about all the raw emotions, the resentments and the betrayals between husbands, wives, sons, daughters, brothers, sisters, and in-laws. These people should be in therapy, not running a company.

Parole Them with Pay

When business owners can't bring themselves to fire incompetent relatives because of some misplaced sense of obligation, we suggest they "Parole Them with Pay." Personally, I'd tell Junior to support himself and find his own job. But if paying him not to show up is what it takes to keep him as far away from your business as possible, it's a worthwhile investment.

I know within minutes of talking to a new client that whatever is not working in the business goes back to a family member. My first clue? When he tells me, "Oh gee, my son is working really hard." Of course he knows he isn't. He's just afraid to admit it. When it comes to family, even the toughest CEOs tiptoe around the issues.

In my business, our senior consultants act as temporary chiefs of operations. That's our niche. We don't file reports. We are implementers. We go to the site, hold the owner's hand, and do the work that needs to be done and isn't getting done because there is a leadership vacuum. When the owner is afraid to confront his kid, we play the parent and tell Timmy to shape up or he's fired.

I remember one job where that was all we had to do: fire three brothers-in-law. We were hired by the three blood brothers who owned a $100 million trucking company in Louisiana. It's not like the business was doing badly. Their father, who was about eighty, had long since retired, leaving his sons equal shares in the business and the authority to run things. It was an ongoing business that had plenty of cash— enough to pay us high six figures to do a job the partners didn't want to do. But if the situation had gone on, they'd be out of business.

The three brothers-in-law were collecting about $200,000 a year each in salary for doing nothing. One brother-in-law was taking kickbacks from the firm's insurance company. Another, in charge of receivables, had about $400,000 in checks on his desk from the previous year that were not deposited because, get this, *he was too lazy to go to the bank!* Another, who was the CFO, was always a year behind in the accounting. His financial statements simply never got done. But every month the company would send the government a check for $1 million, hoping it would cover the assorted taxes and stave off the IRS.

Because of these three brothers-in-law, there were some serious, gaping holes in the operations. The staff all understood what was going on. So did the three owners. But they were afraid to deal with their in-laws because they feared the wrath of their sisters, who'd married these guys for better or worse. That's where we came in. We have no problem firing deadbeats. That's one of the big perks of our job.

We put a new CFO in place, and within a few months the company got a multimillion-dollar tax refund from the IRS. That extra money came in handy for offsetting rising gas costs. The business is also running more efficiently and seeing high double-digit profit growth.

Fire 'Em; They'll Get Over It

As for the brothers-in-law, things were tense at family gatherings for the next year or so. We wanted to have two of the in-laws prosecuted for fraud, but in the end, we backed off. The partners were just happy to be rid of them. Finally, about twelve months later, everyone got together for Thanksgiving dinner, and all was well. The sisters didn't try to poison the three partners' turkey stuffing, and the brothers-in-law were meek as mice.

By the second Thanksgiving, one of the owners called us and said, "That was the best time I ever had, because I didn't have to talk about business at dinner!"

I have the utmost respect for the men and women who've gone out there on their own and built thriving businesses from scratch. People like the business owners I just described are the foundation of our economy. They're living proof that the American dream is possible for anyone willing to put their backs into it and work like maniacs. Small business owners are a breed apart. But they're also human. They can lose everything over a misplaced sense of family loyalty. To sustain a business, control its destiny, and keep the dream alive, they have to suck it up and do the things the average person just isn't willing to do. They have to be willing to fire a family member.

Still don't believe me? I have hundreds of examples of familial incompetence ranging from the comical to the sinister. But they all have the same basic plot line: business loses money; business owner fires the boob he or she is related to; business makes money.

Let me leave you with one final, disturbing example. Lou Mosca, whom you met in Chapter 1, had a job in Connecticut nine years ago, working with a manufacturer of technology equipment that was losing money left and right. The mother and father had worked hard for decades to build up the business, but they were in their mid-sixties and living in Florida eight months of the year. When Lou spent a short time on the site, it became clear that their son was the problem.

Lou is a total pro who never suffers fools. He's a tough Italian-American, born and raised in New York. He isn't a big guy, but his presence fills a room, and one hard look from this guy can make even the most difficult clients fall in line. Nothing impresses him and nothing gets by him. He calls it as he sees it and when he does, you can bet it'll be on the money. The man knows his job and I trust him to make the right decisions when it comes to running a business at peak proficiency.

The parents of this company worked hard for decades to build up the business, but they were getting on in years. They handed the operation over to their only child, whom we'll call "Greg."

As soon as they put their son in charge, things started to go south. They hired us to get to the bottom of the situation and I sent Lou to fill me in.

After an extensive overview of the site, Lou discovered that the loss in revenue was due to Greg's continued mismanagement and general apathy toward properly handling the business. According to some of the employees Lou interviewed, Greg was using the business as his personal, open-ended bank account, spending money on every luxury to which he felt entitled. If you didn't kiss his ring, he became abusive. Lou, being the "get it done" kind of guy he is, approached Greg head-on.

"Tell me, Greg," he said. "What are you contributing in terms of improving profits?"

Greg evaded the question, spewing something about how the company was moving along just fine. Unmoved, Lou continued the line of questioning, determined to expose the holes in the operation, and their cause. He asked about what cash was coming in, from where, and what was going out. Throughout the interview, Greg appeared twitchy and bored, intermittently looking down at his watch while Lou tried to make some sense of the sinking operation. As Lou continued his queries, Greg put up his hand and stopped Lou in mid-sentence. Looking peeved, he stared at Lou and said:

"Who are *you* to tell me how to run my business? I don't have to sit here and listen to this; you work for me!"

Without saying another word, Lou got up, thanked him for his time and walked out. He figured he'd let the kid simmer down and return later to conduct a meeting with all of the owners. In the meantime, he decided to pay a visit to a client who worked in a nearby county. On the way, he got a call from the comptroller at Greg's company, which we'll call "Techies R Us."

"Hello, Lou? This is Melanie. We met earlier today. I'm the comptroller at Techies. Listen, whatever you do, don't come back here tomorrow."

"Why?" Lou asked.

"Greg is fuming! He's running up and down the halls screaming, and he says if he sees you again he's going to kill you. And, sir, he's got a gun."

That was all Lou had to hear. He contacted the state troopers and had them escort him back into the building to confront this pampered maniac. Greg denied the threats and started singing a different tune, claiming he was just cleaning the gun for a friend. No charges were pressed, but Lou called an emergency meeting with the parents and owners and told them about the incident. He told them point blank, "Your son is a cancer to this business; get rid of him!"

Absence Is the Best Family Therapy

Mom and Dad didn't have the heart. They could not confront their son. The project ended and the business deteriorated. Then, about a year and a half later, Lou got a call. They finally took his advice. Today Greg lives far away from his parents and the business, in Wyoming. I assume he found some other company to terrorize. A year after Greg left, Techies R Us realized $800,000 in pure profits. It was the first time in many years the company was out of the red. Meanwhile, the family is getting along just fine.

It's a bad idea, but if you absolutely must continue working with a relative, even after reading these horror stories, NEVER treat them any differently from your other employees. Pay them the same, and expect the same level of performance. And go the extra mile to keep personal issues outside the office.

But my best solution for family members who don't work out is to show them the door. Then change the locks. If you feel you owe them a living, fine. Pay them not to be there. It will be a worthwhile investment to keep them as far away from the premises as possible.

The Best Family Business Has *One* Member

Blood and business don't mix. It's a recipe for office dysfunction.

■

Don't restrict yourself to a pool of untalented brothers, sisters, sons, daughters, or in-laws for key roles. Go outside the bloodline and do a real search for the most qualified job candidates.

■

Gifted members of the lucky sperm club are rare.

■

If you're worried about how Junior is going to pay his bills, parole him with pay, then change the locks on your office door. You'll save money in the end.

■

Firing family members might cause strife, but they'll end up thanking you for creating the legacy of a business that's thriving without them.

Delegate, Don't Abdicate

Two thirds of the business owners we meet delegate important tasks, follow up randomly, and whine when their orders are ignored. They think they should hand over their duties because that's what the HR seminars and management books tell them to do. But what they're not admitting to themselves is that delegating is just another word for shirking responsibility. Expect someone else to do it and 90 percent of the time it won't get done.

Instead, you should wear the badge of "control freak" with pride. Micromanage, micromanage some more, then circle back to make sure the task is getting done, and done right. You may have to put in a lot more time at the office. You'll have to give up a few evenings and most weekends. But you'll ensure your business is making maximum profits. Decide now: Longer hours and more focus, or much less money to put into your bank account? I know which option I'd pick.

Micromanaging is something I do all the time. I have to. Lately there was a problem with the recruiting process at my company (and believe me, we have our share). I knew I had to drill down to the bottom of it. It's essential that we have a fully staffed team of top-notch sales people in the field, and finding those people takes diligence. To keep our sales at full capacity, our recruiters must talk to two or three people an hour to find the right candidate. I started investigating the results of their daily calls. Far too often, the reports stated: "Prospect never called." That had to stop.

The recruiting manager told me they were talking to 75 percent of the job applicants, but a close check revealed that 25 percent was the more accurate number. At the same time, I had my nose in our records on recruiting call connections. I discovered that the outside sales manager was not conducting the final interview before an applicant was selected. These two lapses, plus a general lackadaisical effort, accounted for an overall decline in sales.

It was my problem and my fault. The buck stops with me. I'm the boss. We had a one-sided discussion about the need for improvement. The sales manager was devastated for days that I hadn't kissed him instead of kicking him. In the end, he asked to be relieved of his managerial responsibility. I thought about it for a second and agreed. A new person was put in place, and we're doing much better.

It's all too easy to let things slide. That my company even exists at all is because there is so much dysfunction in small businesses due to owners abdicating responsibility. As I tell our consultants regularly: "If our business owners were doing everything right, you wouldn't have a job."

One of our current clients is a third-generation family-owned car dealership in Tucson, Arizona. The second-generation father put his son and son-in-law in charge so he and his wife could drive across the country in his big new RV and enjoy life. But Dad gave the two men no training and zero support. He owned 100 percent of the stock. He maintained total ownership. But he abdicated. He failed in his own responsibilities and set his son and son-in-law up for failure. He squandered the ability to have oversight in the business, and it was 100 percent his fault.

Things were being so badly managed that one of the major car manufacturers, Chrysler, threatened to pull their brand. It would have meant instant failure. The banks were about to foreclose on the loans, and because Mom and Dad didn't want to be involved and held the purse strings, their kids couldn't get the money necessary to hold the cars they needed to sell in order to maintain revenue and cash flow. The sons were about to lose their homes, because the owner made them sign on with them for the debt.

We brought the father back in for a meeting. We showed him the disaster and, more important, we showed his spouse. Before they went on their extended vacation, the owner hadn't told his wife the kind of financial risk they were taking. He hadn't even told her that the papers he had her sign were to mortgage their home. The business was about to lose everything, and it was her money too. They were headed straight for a box canyon with no money to continue their retirement. That got their attention.

Now he comes in every week to work with us, along with his sons. They told Chrysler they can keep their cars. The brand had been threatening the dealership for years to take it back. It wasn't worth it. It was giving an outsider too much power. With our help, they renegotiated the debt with the bank, transformed the Chrysler lot into a used car location, and refocused their efforts on the Chevy GM brand in the better location. Management merged the best sales people, weeded out the bottom feeders, consolidated costs, and put in tighter controls. The father holds weekly meetings and comes in to show his sons the ropes. Only history will tell us if the third generation is capable enough to take it from there.

The conventional wisdom is that you delegate responsibility and hold people accountable. But in a small business, *you don't have the time or money to correct bad mistakes!* By the time you catch them they could sink sales in your fiscal quarter. It bears repeating that small businesses fail too fast. You have to catch the errors first. Sure, delegate tasks, but watch your employees like a hawk until you are satisfied they are doing what they are supposed to; then keep watching.

Micromanaging Is a Good Thing

It's okay to be a control freak. If we tell a salesperson to make thirty sales calls a day, we shouldn't wait until next Monday to find out the salesperson didn't do it. That employee needs to turn in a report at the end of each day on how many calls were made, to whom, what was said, and when the follow up will happen. You have to be all over it. Sure, let the sales manager, or the financial controller, or the production manager, do their jobs, but be omniscient about it and make sure your orders are followed.

The owner of a $7 million-a-year company in Rhode Island delegated to his CFO the responsibility of dealing with the bank and obtaining a line of credit. He wanted to make sure there was always enough cash flow. But the CFO fudged the receivables. If he collected

$100,000 from a customer, he'd tell the bank he collected $50,000, so the fake numbers would expand the line of credit. We caught it, and the CFO denied it, at first. Then he blamed the owner's wife, and finally pointed the finger at the owner. The CFO got fired, and a year later the company filed for bankruptcy.

It was the owner's fault. Forget blaming the CFO. The boss claimed it was appropriate to have the CFO act on his behalf. We call that the "dummy defense." Somewhere along the line the owner knew it was happening and allowed it to continue because he was distracted by the good life. He was driving a fancy BMW. His wife had a Jaguar. He had a 38-foot Italian speed boat and big RV. He was spending money he didn't have.

This example may be extreme, but it's a variation on a consistent theme. There's a common assumption that micromanaging is somehow a bad thing. We hear owners tell us all the time they need to foster trust with their employees and not second guess them all the time. They believe that if they dole out the extra responsibility their workers will rise to the occasion. Wishful thinking. These are no more than flimsy justifications for being lazy.

Delegate, but Verify

Business owners may think delegation alone is going to lighten their load, but it ultimately creates more work when they have to look under the hood and fix all the damage done while their backs were turned.

Like Ronald Reagan always used to say during the Cold War, "Trust, but verify." At American Management Services, we always say, "Delegate, but verify."

Control at Your Fingertips

Micromanagement makes life easier. With a system of what we call "fingertip controls" in place, a business owner doesn't have to be on-site at all times. Owners can and should be able to do what they want to do, not what they *have* to do. They are entitled to have access to information at all times. Knowledge is control, and control is freedom. That freedom—to be at the cabin on Lake Michigan, or to work out of your ranch in El Paso—comes from being able to dig deep into any department in your organization and know with the click of a mouse your inventory turnover for that day, or the current balance on your checkbook. You should be able to know what is going on in your business, whether it's an operation with a dozen people or five hundred.

After a lifetime of working like a maniac, I am finally in a position to spend my summers in Nantucket and my winters in Palm Beach. Our headquarters are in Orlando, but I still check in numerous times a day. Even though I am not always physically there, I'm proud that my employees still complain they can feel me breathing down their necks. I can access everything I need to know about how my business is functioning on any given day or hour. From the status of my accounts receivables to my expenses and the balance on my line of credit, it just takes a few minutes out of my day to read a one-sheet summary of essential information. I still approve all checks over $500. I can find out in an instant how many checks were written in a given week.

I make sure the telemarketing department sends me reports four times a day on their appointment-setting rate. Those reports—one page documents that contain all crucial details at a glance—are as precise a snapshot of that department as you can get. You must have daily, or at least weekly, "flash" reporting on the vital statistics of all your operating departments and the company as a whole. Fail to get this information at your peril.

Owners should insist on detailed reports on the various flash points of their business. A flash point is that critical nexus in a business where money can be made or lost. It's where the red flag shows up. A perfect example is your checking account. If you've got $50,000 in your account one day, and you're $30,000 overdrawn the next, it's time to start asking questions. Be it sales, production, inventory turnover, or distribution, the longest they should go before drilling down into the critical operations of their business is a week.

It's taken me years of building and adhering to a disciplined business plan to reach the point where I can run my business remotely. Fingertip control has been an essential tool in getting there.

Of course, you still have to be able to trust the people generating those flash reports. Owners need to audit their department heads periodically to make sure they are getting accurate information. Grill those who prepare the reports and get all the details on how they compiled the data. It takes obsessive compulsive commitment and dedication.

Most small business owners have little to no control over the details of their business operations. They have no idea where or how their most critical resources are being used, and inventory-based businesses are among the worst offenders.

We had a client a few years ago who supplied compressed gas to hospitals and clinics throughout the Mid-Atlantic region. Once their customers use up the oxygen or other compressed substances, they have to return the special steel canisters to our client for refilling. But no one, from the owner to the inventory manager, had a clue where those canisters were, or how many were off-site.

Every year they were spending high six-figure sums on new canisters they wouldn't need with the proper inventory controls in place. In a business that should have been making a 12 percent profit margin, they were getting by on 1.6 percent. This business was losing $1.5 million a year of profit, and about half of those losses, or $750,000, was due to the added and unnecessary expense of purchasing new canisters.

This owner abdicated responsibility, claiming inventory control was the job of the general manager. The general manager said he was managing inventory the way it was always done, or not done. But it was easier to know where the canisters were when the business only supplied one or two locations. Now the business was supplying to customers spread across ten states!

As always, problems in the business were multiple, but lack of inventory control was the owner's most expensive mistake. It was also the easiest to correct. We put fingertip controls in place, with detailed computer tracking of how many canisters were at client sites. The general manager operated the new tracking system, but we made sure the owner knew it was HIS responsibility to stay on top of it. Within months, his profit margin grew another eleven percentage points.

Willful ignorance of the details of an operation is a surefire recipe for its demise. A perfect example of this mindset occurred four years ago when Lou was on-site with a company in Ohio, a $30 million-a-year distributor of industrial cleaning supplies. Lou got into a fierce argument with the owner. This guy wanted to fire Lou and our team of consultants on the spot, because we were poking around the shipping and receiving department a little too much for his liking. But we had to. Something didn't smell right. The flow of paperwork seemed off somehow. There were too many cash leaks. We were determined to find the source.

The business owner had handed full responsibility for shipping and receiving to a longtime employee and friend. When Lou started questioning this employee's role, the CEO said:

"He's been with me forever. Leave him alone or you're outta here!"

Now, it would have been easy enough to play by his rules and collect our fee. But Lou stood his ground.

"Okay, Joe, how about this? I make a few discreet inquiries and if it's nothing, I'll back right off," Lou said.

The guy relented. In the face of hard facts, he had no choice. We found out the shipping manager was fabricating bills of lading for shipments. When something got shipped in, he'd write up a double invoice—one from the vendor and the other from his own side business. Meanwhile, his boss was getting double-billed to the tune of $400,000 over two years. This shipping manager, confident he was untouchable, had a friend in the accounts department help him process the checks. That was easy enough to do, because the boss only had to approve checks cut for more than $5,000. It was a cozy setup.

When Lou presented the business owner with the evidence, it hit the fan. We opened his eyes to an unpleasant reality. Then we brought in a sheriff and an attorney, and had the shipping manager arrested for fraud.

The owner could have stepped in before the losses occurred. By handing over total authority to the head of a department that was critical to his business, with no oversight, he allowed himself to be robbed blind. And there is no question he should have been signing off on all orders over $500. But he abdicated to a longtime favorite employee, and would have been happy to live in denial until we came along. Had Lou not insisted on doing his job, you can be sure the business would have bled dry in no time.

Trust No One!

Theft is the biggest risk to business owners who delegate to the point of abdication. They make it so easy for less ethical employees. It's tantamount to leaving an open wallet full of cash on the table and walking away. A classic example of this kind of naïve neglect took place two years ago, when a construction client in Illinois hired a chief of operations and gave him full control over the daily operations of all the branches.

The father and son owners had turned their backs on the business, figuring this guy, who was qualified and talked a good game, had it all under control. He sure did. He even starting putting the above-mentioned fingertip controls in place, except that they were slapdash and solely for the benefit of his own sticky fingers. The owners let the COO run things his way for nine months, until complaints from various branch managers started pouring in. That's when we got the call.

Our immediate advice was to throw this guy out on his keister. The next step was to hire a private eye, who went on to uncover that every time the COO paid a visit to one of the branch locations he was wining and dining his mistress and staying at five-star hotels, all at the company's expense. Employees at the seventeen branch offices didn't even see him when he was in town. He was too busy working the company credit card to do his job. The guy was getting paid $200,000 a year, plus he was racking up another $200,000 in expenses, and he managed to squeeze another $24,000 for his BMW, which he already paid for in cash. He turned company expenses into his own personal racket. Not only did the firm wind up paying in excess of $400,000 for a deadweight employee, it lost over $2 million in sales during his tenure. It was all the evidence we needed. We fired the freeloader.

Then we made the owner hire a hard line, no nonsense CFO, and put real controls in place. But we made sure that it was the father and son, not the CFO, who received and read the flash reports. I don't care what kind of superstar resume an employee has, NEVER hand them the reins. There is just too much money at stake. When it comes to cash, trust no one.

Prepare for Disaster

You may think you already run a tight ship. Maybe you show up every day and dedicate long hours to making sure your business functions smoothly. That's commendable. But imagine what would happen if you couldn't be on-site day after day. God forbid it should happen to you, but sometimes circumstances force a business owner to delegate. That doesn't have to spell disaster if a proper system of controls is in place.

We're working with a client in Virginia who owns a 20,000-square-foot exotic pet store. I'm not talking about some shop that sells budgies and hamsters. This place sells $15,000 boa constrictors, $10,000 Japanese coi, exotic birds, tarantulas, you name it. This guy got into the business because he loves animals, and he was making tidy profits in the high six figures. Then, a little over two years ago, he got into a terrible motorcycle accident. Just about every bone in his body was smashed. He had nineteen separate surgeries and he was off work for six months. He was so physically debilitated he had no choice but to abdicate.

While he was out of commission his staff, the "loyal team" who had been working at the store forever, took it upon themselves to hire extra help. Everyone made their own lives better while the boss recovered in the hospital. Four staff members on the night shift became nine. Worker productivity was cut in half. They were running the store like a country club. Employees saw themselves as saving endangered species, fussing more over how to take care of the iguanas rather than selling them.

Now the rent is in arrears. With no reporting to hold people accountable, theft has become an issue, cash flow is nonexistent, state sales taxes haven't been paid, the line of credit is about to get cut, and the owner is so far behind in paying the bills that the electric company is about to pull the plug.

The owner is still struggling to put a system in place. He brought us in because he is facing bankruptcy, and frankly I'm still not sure if we can save him (more on this in Chapter 11). Three weeks into the job we've slashed payroll, created incentive plans for the salespeople, renegotiated terms with all the vendors, and gotten a three-month abatement on rent from the landlord. We're doing our best to shore up cash. He has a fighting shot if he can get through the next holiday season. Exotic pet sales tend to pick up in the spring, when wealthy customers buy new coi for their ponds.

But our biggest problem right now is the owner. After the trauma he went through, watching the business he built on his back crumble into this mess has been more than he can take. Our consultants keep trying to lift this poor guy up so he'll battle through another day, but most of the time he just sits with his head in his hands and sobs. He is continuing to abdicate because of his fragile mental state.

And the tragedy of all this is that it didn't have to happen this way. With the proper fingertip controls already in place, there would be no question of abdication. He could have run the business from his hospital bed.

Never let go of control. Once you do, the price may be too high and you might never get back what you had.

Delegate, Don't Abdicate

Micromanage, and micromanage some more.

■

Don't delegate to the point of abdication. Catch the errors before they happen, because bad mistakes are too costly in small business.

■

Use flash reports: one-sheeters that give you daily updates on the status of each flashpoint in your business.

■

Delegate, but verify. Trust no one.

■

Never hand over the reins, no matter how senior the employee.

■

Wear your control freak badge with pride!

PROFIT RULE 7

Live and Die by a Real Plan

Owners always say they have a financial and operating plan, but few do. Most of these are on the back of an envelope or gathering dust in the bottom drawer, never to see the light of day again. Some owners say they have one in their head, but it only serves to clutter their brains. Most of these plans are never reviewed or modified, and changes are rarely implemented.

Stop Fibbing That You Have One

If you don't have a strong and evolving plan for profits, don't bother to come to work, because you will fail. Running your business month-to-month, week-to-week, and day-to-day, you'll always be playing catch-up to meet expenses. But if you choose to live by our creed that "profits are the ONLY thing," then a disciplined plan is the only way you are going to get there. You should be focused about where you stand on your plan every hour that you're working and implement the required changes without mercy.

Profits Last

Most companies estimate sales, then go department by department to figure out the cost of those sales before arriving at the bottom number: the profit. Profit comes last. It is on the bottom of the income statement, effectively making it last on the list of priorities. And that is an unacceptable way of running your business if you care about making real money.

Owners who pretend to have a real plan use this kind of "residual budgeting," usually resulting in no profits, or worse, losses. They are budgeting operations on hope and failing to adjust accordingly when they fail to meet their projections or the market tanks. Failing to react immediately when budgets get out of line leads to disaster.

Even the most detailed and active operating plans should be tossed out in favor of what we call a *Profits First* plan. Most companies prepare a budget operating plan by estimating sales levels, usually too optimistically. They then determine what costs they think they need to achieve their profit goal at year end. Their profits become the leftovers of their sales and operating expenses. We refer to this tendency as a residual profit plan, and I've rarely seen one where the sales are realistic estimates. They are dreams and wind up falling apart at the seams, imperiling both profits and continued financing from the bank.

Small business owners must be fanatical about living by a Profits First plan. This operating plan depends on an owner's commitment to be in the top quartile of their industry. Average in the bottom quartile doesn't work for me, and shouldn't work for you.

If You're Not Trying to Be the Best You Can Be, Pack It In!

Owners rarely make enough changes to keep the bottom-line profits intact. They avoid the issue, allowing apathy to get in the way of fiscal discipline. Instead of making the necessary cuts as sales deteriorate, they tell themselves they'll make it up in the next quarter. This adds up to disaster.

The conventional, residual budget plan permits these lax cost controls. If we take a specialty manufacturing company with $8 million in expected sales, for example, the owner overestimates sales for the upcoming quarter or year and determines his or her best guess at expenses. The owner then comes up with a profit of $500,000. But that figure is purely abstract and almost never realized. As sales deteriorate, especially in a recessionary market, profits and cash flow rapidly disappear.

15 Cents for You, 85 Cents for the Business

Taking this same company, we would use our Profits First plan and reduce the sales to $7 million. Assuming the industry top quartile of a 15 percent profit rate, the company's operating profit should be $1.05 million. Our operating plan puts those anticipated Profits First, leaving the expense budget at $5.95 million. Ownership must then make sure all expense levels are planned and controlled to the expense budget of $5.95 million. All expenses, from sales commissions to general and administrative expenses, even rent, cannot exceed that expense budget of $5.95 million. Simply put, the company has to run on $5.95 million and expenses must be cut if they are too high going into the new year.

By doing this, by making sure your expenses going into the new year do not exceed that amount, your operating profit will be in the industry upper quartile at $1.05 million, and that's after you pay yourself a realistic salary of $175,000 to $250,000. You are taking your profit first and making sure 15 cents on every dollar goes to the house first, rather than to operating expenses. An extreme would be to take 15 cents of every dollar that you collect and put it in a separate bank account, to be used only for capital investment or other non-operating costs.

Our Profits First approach is the only concrete way you can ensure and measure performance among your departments and individual employees. Set a clear profit target, stick to a prescribed budget, and teach management how to hold everyone accountable, both operationally and financially. Each department head, and each individual within that department, needs to be given a timeline for completion of tasks, which must be performed successfully and within budget. Everyone, from the top down, must be held to a minimum and measurable standard of performance that supports this business plan. And if you don't viciously control costs according to this plan, you'll slide into razor-thin profit margins—or losses.

No room for muddy math here. With a Profits First plan in place, management has no excuse for failure, because the financial and operational goals of your business are all laid out by the numbers at the beginning of the year. Your employees have clear marching orders, which you can refer back to again and again.

In a bad year, this is a lifesaver. Let's assume that your marketing and sales costs under this plan were originally $700,000, but sales have dipped 10 percent below your budget. You then have to adjust your future sales costs to meet the new reality of lower sales so the percentage of sales costs against your new cost figure ($5,525,000) stays the same. This Profits First plan automatically forces a reduction in your sales costs and other operating expenses. By doing so, your 15 percent profit figure is maintained regardless of the sales drop. But if you don't execute the cost cuts in your sales budget and other factors, you will not meet the profit expectation in your plan.

Reheat the Leftovers

Profits First works for any industry. If you open a Chinese restaurant tomorrow, which statistically makes 12 percent profits, you set aside the first 12 cents of every dollar and run the business on the remaining 88 cents. If you are a contractor and the industry makes 8 percent pretax, take 8 percent off what your sales are going to be. Make money first and pay your expenses second, so you take the first 8 cents of every dollar that comes into your business, and pay salaries and other operating costs out of the remaining 92 cents.

Expose Your Profit Leaks

There are countless advantages to this Profits First system of budgeting. Installing this system reveals where each unit of a business is overspending, because it forces business owners to end denial by regularly scrutinizing and adjusting costs.

Seven years ago we worked with a company in Nevada that made trailers for hauling landscape equipment. The business was doing $5 million in sales, and their profits were consistently at zero. Two years before we got there the company was losing $100,000 a year.

We installed a Profits First plan, which called for the same sales level and an annual profit of $500,000. The owner thought we were crazy and believed he could never make that much money. We knew better.

The business had three locations so we set up a Profits First system at each site, with the goal of reducing operating costs. When we ran the numbers at each branch we discovered the newest location was all cost and no return. Customers at the third branch could be serviced from the other locations. As it turns out, the owner had opened the third site for the ego gratification of building large volume, but the extra capacity was fiscal suicide. We had the owner close that location, which increased volume at the other two sites. By using our Profits First budget, the losing location stuck out like a sore thumb. By closing it and cutting other costs, the business's profits soared 9 percent to $450,000 on the same sales.

Hundreds of business owners see sales volume as a sign of success. But Profits First leaves no room for self-delusion. Or deceit. Concentrating on unprofitable sales just masks overall losses.

In 2005 we worked with a $14 million distributor of paper and packaging in Oregon that was consistently losing about $250,000 each year because the two brothers who owned the business did not know the right or wrong level of expense for each department. Overspending was rampant. This oversight opened the door for some not quite kosher travel and credit card expenses, costing the company tens of thousands of dollars a year.

We forced the two brothers to go through their profit and loss statement and justify why each item had to exist. The one line item that stood out was inventory. They were overbuying materials, wiping out profit, and pushing the business deep into the red.

Sloppy budgeting and excessive purchasing weren't the only issues. We met a lot of resistance to the Profits First plan from one brother, who happened to be pushing far too many personal credit card purchases through as travel expenses. The meetings got heated and he tried to throw our consultants under a bus, claiming the new budgeting system was too restrictive. But in our experience, whenever someone resists obvious improvements in financial management, they've got something to hide.

Ruthless enforcement of Profits First, because it focuses on costs, can be a great tool in uncovering any funny business. We held that brother's feet to the fire and he confessed. He realized his own short-sighted greed was getting in the way of making bigger money for the ownership. Since then the two brothers, by focusing on Profits First and taking no prisoners, achieved a $1 million swing to profitability, making 6 percent on $16 million in sales.

We make certain that every one of our clients has a Profits First plan in place before we finish the engagement. We have never seen one being used before we get there. Sacrificing operating expenses for the sake of profits is an alien concept to most business owners. But as soon as they see the benefits, they embrace it.

Learn to Live Without

It's all about discipline. You've got to hold yourself accountable for profits and adjust costs daily, weekly, and monthly. You'd be amazed at how easily you can adapt and adjust to minor trims along the way. No cost in business is truly fixed. There's plenty you can learn to live without.

Profits First is like the family that says, "Okay, we are going to save $1,000 a month and go without until we can put that $1,000 into our savings account." It's a whole different mindset. It's a way of approaching financial operations that ensures costs don't get out of control.

Budget with an Iron Fist

Seven years ago we worked with a bus distributor in Arkansas that was dying. Revenue had eroded from $11 million to less than $6 million a year. The business was operating at a steep loss, and had about another year to live.

The owner, we'll call him "Pete," was an engaging, entrepreneurial type in his mid-forties. He started as a parts distributor twenty years ago and built his business up from scratch. Pete had a great attitude and he was doing a lot of things right. He always ate his vegetables first. He was determined and hardworking, and eager to learn. A true fighter. But his system of accounting was all wrong.

Over the years, as Pete was growing and expanding his business, his debt load grew out of control. On top of excessive capital investments, his operational costs weren't being managed for profit. Meanwhile, Pete had hitched his wagon to one primary vendor who represented 50 percent of sales. That vendor shut down without notice, putting the business into crisis.

But the deeper problem was Pete's fuzzy arithmetic when it came to operating expenses. Not living by Profits First put his business in a position of extreme vulnerability. There was just no making up for the sudden cutback in orders. Increased sales would require drastic product expansion or diversification of his customer base, and Pete just didn't have the cash on hand to make it happen. That money was already spent, and then some. He needed to work with what little resources he had to climb out of the hole he found himself in.

We convinced him to start with a Profits First plan in the service department—the part of the business that appeared to be leaking the most cash. The business was way behind on job orders and overspent on equipment and supplies it didn't need. The garage space was half empty and at least a quarter of the staff was idle. A Profits First plan uncovered these holes.

We taught the department head and every employee in that department how to break down spending month by month, make adjustments, and adhere to the profit plan we set forth. Often, that's all it takes. When workers have no clear direction, when there is no transparency, and they have to second guess what the boss wants and the business needs, they fall behind. But a clear-cut goal changes that dynamic. By the first month, the department had a surplus of cash.

Seeing how well the new system was working, Pete asked us to implement Profits First throughout the company. We repeated the training in the sales department, the new and used departments, and the parts department.

The new system weeded out the management and employees who didn't want to be held accountable. The service department manager quit, and so did the assistant manager. That's exactly what we wanted. We hired new blood and these managers were more than willing to be responsible for results, because they knew if they outperformed expectations, they'd also be rewarded. (More on this in the next chapter.)

Cut Ruthlessly to Earn

The fiscal discipline that Profits First demands is the *only* way to survive in a turbulent economy. You might not be able to grow your sales, but you can still earn a profit if you and your employees stick religiously to the plan.

Five years ago we worked with a $16 million private ambulance company outside Portland, Oregon where profits were erratic and mediocre at best. One year the business would make $1 million in profit, the next it would net $200,000. The owners claimed it was impossible to predict and control operating costs. Insurance costs were skyrocketing, and fender benders and traffic and safety violations cost the company hundreds of thousands of dollars each year.

We told them they were going to net 10 percent on their profits, no matter what. Once that absolute number, $1.6 million, was fixed in their heads, they could focus on ways to cut costs and make themselves much more money. We implemented training and safety programs for drivers, along with trip reporting, and installed tracking devices in each ambulance. Each employee would be put on a monthly payout plan that would reward them based on a point system for following safety protocols and bringing insurance costs down. It worked. The company has maintained 10 percent profit margins ever since.

It always works. Three years ago we worked with a $15 million cement manufacturer and distributor in North Dakota that was doing okay, with profit margins of about 5 percent, but management wanted to do better. Ownership had transferred from the father to his two sons, and they wanted to maintain a level of performance in the company regardless of the ups and downs of the market place. We had them set a profit target of 8 percent and made it the responsibility of each department manager to set standards for their staff to hit their budgets consistently. They created specific job descriptions and timelines for execution, making sure to reward employees who delivered within the budget. Today the company nets 8 percent in an industry that's getting crushed. While other construction companies go out of business, this owner is making it work even as sales go down.

That result is well worth the effort of implementing an aggressive Profits First plan.

Live & Die by the Plan

Think about where you stand on your financial
and operating plan every day of the week.

■

Estimate your profits for the year ahead and set that money aside.

■

15 cents profit for you; 85 cents for the business. Or 10 cents and
90 . . . whatever the top of your industry standard happens to be.

■

Put Profits First always.
Don't accept the mere leftovers or residual budgeting.

■

If you're having a bad year, adjust expenses accordingly and
never spend beyond the original plan. Save to earn.

■

Let employees know the plan and hold them
accountable to it. Give them financial incentives to
exceed expectations for budgets and timelines.

■

Clear up the muddy math and expose your profit leaks.

PROFIT RULE 8

Pay for Performance

No more pay raises. Freeze your salaries now. Pay for performance is an absolute necessity for small and midsized businesses to achieve real profitability, and big money for the owner. It is so important to determining the success or failure of your business that if you don't install pay for performance today, you should fire yourself.

We hear plenty of talk about pay for performance in large corporations, and the term is widely used to describe small, incremental bonuses. Typically, in their version of pay for performance if someone makes, say, $30,000 a year, they can make another $3,000 in bonus pay.

But, in my view, that's nowhere near enough to create performance incentive. We believe that anywhere from 30 percent to 100 percent of an employee's compensation should be based on performance, both good and bad, and that amount should be against the goals set for employees by the owner.

Adjust Accordingly

Pay for performance means exactly that. You are compensating your employees according to how well, or how poorly, they perform. It's not some year-end bonus that everybody gets if the company does well. It's your employees' livelihood, and it goes up and down depending on how they meet or exceed the goals you've set for them.

All employees, from the shop floor manager to the accounting and administrative departments, should be on some form of pay for performance. Obviously, that percentage can vary, depending on whether you are an executive assistant or a head of sales. But everyone contributes or detracts in some way to the bottom line, whether they are saving costs by keeping a sharp eye on inventory, saving you valuable time by being an efficient executive assistant, or holding up the entire business by filing a report three days late. It's a matter of tailoring the type of pay for performance so it's relevant to each type of employee.

But this profit rule applies especially to businesses with sales staff. Salespeople should have 100 percent of their compensation based on pay for performance. We regularly see clients who pay their sales employees a salary no matter how they perform, and it makes no sense. I guarantee you won't see your sales manager hanging around the office past five on a Friday if he gets his check regardless. If he had a bad week and accomplished little in sales, he'll just shrug it off, make excuses, and tell himself he'll do better next week. Either way, you'll be shelling out and getting mediocrity in return. But a sales manager whose entire financial week depends on making those sales numbers will push and push and push, because it's her pocket too.

We worked with a printing company in Pennsylvania that had

everyone on a salary and, of course, its profits were in a trough. We immediately put the outside sales team on a 100 percent pay for performance, and 30 percent pay for performance for the inside sales support team. The sales manager wouldn't buy into a commission-based program and left, along with several others. But it was easy enough to find new recruits willing and able to get aggressive about sales. The company was better off without the ones who left.

The client recently came back to me and said it was the best change he ever made. He went from 60 percent productivity to a workforce operating on all cylinders five days a week. Sales rose 30 percent in a business that is almost historically defunct. He's making bigger profits because costs are lower and the sales force is more focused and happier, because they're generating more income for themselves. By installing variable commissions, the owner is even scaling compensation to the profitability of each product sold, driving the pay for performance program in targeted ways that boost the bottom line.

Hit Them Where It Counts!

Pay for performance doesn't just mean an employee gets paid more for doing well. This is not just an entitlement. You've got to be willing to slap workers on the side of the head, or the wallet, if they fail to perform assigned tasks in a timely manner. This is controversial. Many so-called management gurus insist that punishing underperformance is de-motivating, and that pay for performance should only entail a positive reward. Most business owners get squeamish about negative reinforcement. But if your check is lower on Friday, you'll be darn sure not to make the same mistake next week. You have to be willing to set up a system that penalizes failure to perform. It's critical to the success of a pay for performance program.

I practice what I preach and believe me, it works. One of my biggest pet peeves (and there are many) is when my employees fail to stay in touch with headquarters. We started American Management Services back in the 1980s, when there were no handheld computers and cell phones were rare. We relied on beepers, which our field staff often ignored. I can't count how many times I'd be told the beeper fell in the pool or got run over by a truck. I started docking people $50 when they failed to return a call within thirty minutes. I never heard those lame excuses again.

It also makes me nuts when members of my consulting team fail to submit their weekly billings. It slows down the accounting department. Indeed, it slows down the whole train. So if the reports are not in by Monday morning, the consultants are docked $25. You can bet we don't have that problem any more.

The same goes for collecting checks from clients. I've stopped issuing my sales team advances against commissions. It's up to them to bring in the cash by Monday morning if they want to get paid. Doug McDermod, my head of consulting operations who's been with me forever, was so fearful of being "that guy," he went to heroic lengths to make sure he always collected on time. When he found out on Friday that three of his client checks somehow ended up in the trash, he spent the weekend on the phone begging clients to reissue the checks, then got in his car at 5 a.m. on Monday to drive all over New England to pick them up. He had them turned into the accounts department by 10 o'clock that same morning.

Money Talks

You can use pay for performance to motivate anyone, even unionized workers. Five years ago we had a client up in New Hampshire—a construction contractor that erected metal roofing and wall structures—and this business was hemorraging on job sites.

The owner of the business started the company with his grandfather back in 1987, when he was just in his twenties. This guy worked in the field and learned his trade from the bottom up. He had great skills in the operations side of the business. But when he bought his grandfather out, he began to realize he had no clue about financial management. The business was growing beyond his ability to control it. Projects were ongoing, without any budget or performance metrics. The owner would go out every day and run as fast as he could, but lack of accountability was costing the $5 million business more than 12 percent in productivity and man-hours. He was losing money fast.

For his first meeting at the client site, Doug was sent to the old Sears building on Kenmore Square in Boston. He got there at 5:30 on a freezing cold morning in January and climbed up to the interior of the seventh floor by 5:45 to find the field superintendent and his workers sitting around drinking coffee. By 6:30 they were STILL drinking coffee, so Doug asked, "What's the deal? Why aren't your men working?"

Doug was told that it was still too dark to work at 6 a.m. because daylight hadn't broken yet. This seemed reasonable enough, except the men were bailing out at 2:30 p.m. because they wanted to beat the rush-hour traffic. That meant they were working seven hours a day instead of the eight they were paid for. The job had eight workers, so that was eight man-hours a day lost, at union wages, at a total cost of tens of thousands of dollars for each project.

We had the owner set the hours from 7 a.m. to 3:30 p.m. and established daily productivity goals for each worker. The project superintendents were put on pay for performance. They were paid on the percentage of the value of the hours saved on a job. That meant they could earn between 10 percent and 25 percent more on their base wage, so they were more than happy to take the deal.

Within a year, profits doubled on the same volume of work. Within five years, sales doubled and profits doubled again. The number of employees has also grown, from forty to seventy, but with the fat cut out of the pay, they are earning their keep and then some.

The consensus has long been that it's all but impossible to implement pay for performance in the construction business because of the aggressive and unruly nature of workers, especially when they are unionized. But that's a copout. Enabling workers to do better and make more money works in any industry. Everyone wants to earn more. Now this construction company has a profit margin of 10 percent, twice the industry standard, despite a bleak construction market.

You Can't Have the Carrot Without the Stick

Of course, the devil is in the details. You can't just hand employees a lump of cash at the end of the year. As I mentioned earlier, each program has to be tailored to the needs of the business and its various departments.

Last year we worked with a $25 million high tech machine shop in Minnesota using pay for performance, but it was having no impact on staff because it was done only at the end of the year. The carrot was so far out in the future that the value was lost and employees couldn't relate to it. The payout was only loosely tied to the overall bonus, and people viewed it as an entitlement.

Attitudes among employees were lax. In an industry where labor, parts, and material are extremely expensive, deadlines weren't being met and they were going over budget. When goals weren't met, the department managers would make excuses and finger point in the daily morning meetings. There were profit leaks all over the place and the failure to collect on billings was hurting cash flow every month. As a result, profits were hurting and sales were slowing down.

We put the entire company on a pay for performance plan, measuring each department against financial performance metrics monthly and reviewing each employee quarterly. Four times a year, workers receive written documents detailing what they did well and what they failed to deliver, whether it was an incomplete assignment or a missed deadline. We call it a "Deficiency Notice." These real-life examples of failure to complete a task are then tied to how much an employee receives out of the pay for performance pool predetermined at the beginning of each fiscal year. In other words, employees start off the year with a full account, and when they mess up or fail to improve, it costs them. You wouldn't believe the difference it makes.

Today, workers show up for the daily production meeting at 6:45 a.m. fully prepared with questions and concerns. The owner leads the meeting with a whiteboard and black marker in his hand, outlining examples of profit leaks and underperformance, teaching and motivating employees to correct the flaws so they don't cost the company or come out of their paychecks. Each department is fully aware of financial management goals and their responsibility for meeting them. Staff members willingly work late, and everyone puts in a minimum half day on Saturday.

Yes, you can and must make these demands of your employees. You can't change workers' salaries without explaining it in writing first.

Those who refuse may decide to get off the train. It happens. But those aren't the ones you want to keep. Smart and capable workers will see an opportunity for themselves and go for it. They'll be more dedicated and loyal to the business than you ever thought possible.

Chop the Deadwood

Extraordinary performers should be paid extraordinarily well, but middle of the road workers had better improve fast. Get rid of the deadwood and replace it. Sure, let them know where they stand and give them a chance to get better, but don't tolerate mediocrity.

Remember the GE days when the bottom third was going to be churned? Jack Welch should be a pussycat compared to you. Do NOT tolerate mediocrity. You can't afford to.

This practice works. You're not going to lose good people, because pay for performance bonuses allow workers to make more. Or less, if they fail to deliver. I hear some of you asking yourselves, "Yes, but many valuable employees prefer the job security of a set salary." Here's a newsflash: There IS no job security. Pay for performance ultimately allows for more certainty because each employee can prove, by the numbers, exactly how his or her performance contributes to the bottom line, and NO small business owner is going to lay off someone who helps the company make money.

I don't care if it's a waiter, a receptionist, or the guy in the mailroom, pay them a low base salary and reward them for a job well done. Every employee who contributes is going to be happy. As for the rest, who cares? If they don't have the drive they don't deserve to be there. It's not your role as the business owner to subsidize laziness.

A recent case in point is a car dealership in New York state that employed a sales manager, a service manager, and a parts manager. They were all getting paid comfortable salaries. But business was flat.

On a Thursday the consultant on the job, Lou Mosca, asked the sales manager for his plan to grow sales. The guy said, "I'll have it for you by Monday." The following Monday night, the sales manager came into the dealership, pulled out two bar napkins from his pocket, and said, "Here's the sales plan. We're going to spend a lot of money on advertising in week one; sell a lot of cars in weeks two and three; then coast along until the next month."

Lou stared at him in disbelief. When it dawned on him that the sales manager was being serious, he asked him what his sales target was. The previous month, the guy had sold nineteen cars. His plan was to up that number to twenty. Lou said that wasn't good enough, to which the sales manager replied, "The problem with you guys is that you're never happy with anything." He quit two days later.

That sales manager was getting paid a full salary of $80,000 with no pay for performance. Good riddance.

Pay for Performance

No more raises. Freeze your salaries now.

■

Everyone should be on 30 percent to 100 percent
pay for performance, especially your outside sales team.

■

The whiners can walk. The winners know they'll make more
money this way, and they're the ones you want to keep.

■

Fire and hire faster. Don't tolerate mediocrity.

■

Review performance monthly and quarterly
and adjust pay accordingly. Pay for performance
isn't some year-end bonus entitlement.

■

Don't be shy about deducting points for failure to deliver.
Hit 'em where it counts: in their wallets.

"I Am Your Work God"

YOU'VE GOT TO BE a tyrant. Owning a small business isn't a popularity contest. You cannot be effective as the owner of a business unless you are feared and respected by your employees. There's no point in managing by the numbers or having a precise operational plan for profits unless you are willing to enforce, enforce, enforce.

This chapter is about an attitude. You've got to demand what you want. Owners generally don't do this. They read books on sensitivity and ingratiate themselves with everyone. They want to be friends and colleagues. Iron rule makes them squeamish. They operate under the mistaken but widely held belief that they'll get more out of their employees if they're liked.

Forget your likeability score. Let your employees fear and respect you first.

My view tends to trample conventional wisdom. The "Lovey-Dovey" school of employee relations might work in some big business, but rarely does it work on Main Street. The "School of Tough Love" is the only way to go. You can get away with a lovey-dovey approach with an exuberant economy, sometimes, but more often than not it ensures jobs don't get done and performance at all levels is mediocre at best. These days, you can't afford to be nice. Your employees won't thank you for being tough on them, but at the end of the day they'll respect the dictator who keeps the business afloat and continues to cut them a monthly paycheck.

It may sound obvious to some of you, but in today's warm, fuzzy, and politically correct environment, where it's all about collaboration, fairness, and listening to your employees, many small business owners forget one important thing: they have a business to run. This ain't a democracy. The only opinion that matters is your own.

I'm a big proponent of the "Just View Me as God" school of management. Not long ago we had an incident at American Management Services where we weren't gathering appropriate and critical information about our clients. We struck down into the ranks of our administrators and held a video conference call when I defined how we wanted this information gathered. I told them to think of me as God. Everyone laughed, but they also knew I meant it. We imposed economic penalties on our field personnel if the information was not received timely and appropriately. The information problem has not occurred since.

In the 6,000 small businesses we've worked with, the dictatorial and tough love school of management far surpasses whatever comes second. Ignore the human resources gurus who preach patience, calm, civility, and multiple warnings. You can't afford to waste your time repeating yourself and losing the money that poor follow through from your employees can cause.

Don't Think, Obey

I want my employees to do what I say, not what they think. As a manager I don't have the time to keep repeating instructions. I believe too much is lost by allowing employees to disregard special instructions because they think they have a better way. I don't want them to try to shade what has to be done. They can view me any way they want on their own time, but when they're on my clock, I want them to take my word as an absolute decree. If they do what I say, they can go home happy and job-secure.

It's about what the company needs, not what the employee wants. Put policies and procedures in place and explain them once. Make sure everyone toes the line. If your workers are dodging their half of the deal and still expecting to get paid, they shouldn't be there. You can't brook any deviation, because as soon as you allow that to happen the inmates are running the asylum. Before you know it you'll be losing lots of money.

Take No Prisoners

Always run by the numbers and be tyrannical about enforcing them. Every time you let up, a profit leak can become a gusher. Produce an estimated financial statement weekly; analyze and agonize about it on Saturday, and restore profitability on Monday.

Three years ago we worked with a $7 million contractor just outside of Little Rock, Arkansas who installed heating, ventilation, and air conditioning systems. He was losing money because he was not managing his business, or his people, by the numbers. Instead, his people were running him. There was no daily reporting of hours in the field, and if workers didn't see the next job coming they'd drag their feet on the current project to extend it to meet their own payroll needs. They wouldn't call into the office to update the status. If a job wasn't finished, they wouldn't stay a couple more hours to finish. As a result, the owner couldn't tell if the overtime reported was over budget or under budget. There was no accountability and no control.

The owner was a nice guy who depended on his employees to do the right thing. He wanted his people to love him, and he didn't want to enforce things he knew needed to be enforced. It wasn't necessarily the employees' fault the company was out of cash. They took advantage of the owner's lax management style and loose controls because they could. The prevailing attitude was, "Hey, I'm getting my paycheck every week, so what do I care?" The owner opened the door to that behavior by choosing to be Mr. Popularity over Mr. Profits.

When we got there we created a series of daily and weekly reports that accounted for all employee activities. The hours had to be reported daily and compared against the budget. Managers had to be responsible for getting field people back in when they completed the work, not when the employee felt it was necessary.

Over a few months, the owner's attitude changed from wanting to be liked to wanting to be respected. He realized that as the boss he couldn't afford to accept squishy answers or performance. He insisted upon enforcing the new rules. Hundreds of man-hours were saved and volume doubled. He went from losses to a respectable 10 percent profit margin.

Being a tyrant by itself isn't enough. You've got to be meticulous about knowing your corporate financial status at all times. Define your expectations of employees and set up an airtight process to hold them accountable. If you can't define accountability for an employee, you probably don't need them.

We worked with a business owner, a successful roofer in Minneapolis, who was an above-average operational tyrant. He built up a team of long-term employees. When he hired new staff, he screened them relentlessly and let them know they would only get to work with him once. If they resigned they'd never be rehired. He was up front about what he wanted. He told everyone he wanted them to know what they didn't know, and learn it. Workers were expected to show up for the daily morning meeting at 6:45 a.m., sharp, and they did.

But despite the owner's tough principles, he lacked a system of accountability that was tied to the end game: profits. These were long-term, loyal employees, but they were underperforming because they'd reached a point where they couldn't grow any more in the organization. They needed to be challenged to generate more business and meet increasingly higher financial and management goals.

We installed rational measures of performance tied to the profit plan of the organization. The managers had to examine where their departments were financially and operationally at the end of each month, and be steps ahead of the owner in suggesting ways to pick up the pace of production and operate within budgets and deadlines. From order entry, through purchasing and production, each manager was under the gun to execute the production process and have the next job ready to roll when the last job ended. They had to be ready with suggestions for improvements when something went wrong, and finger pointing and excuses would not be tolerated.

The owner was already halfway there with his tough, unapologetic approach. But by defining and communicating his financial and operational expectations with a precise plan, he earned more than just the respect of his employees: He won himself an iron fist full of dollars.

Excuses Are Irrelevant!

Most of our clients aren't even close to being tyrants. They permit their employees to walk all over them. Even when they try to lay down the law, they cave in at the first flimsy excuse.

There are obvious exceptions, like a death in the immediate family. If, for example, your accounts receivable administrator's father dies and she needs to take some time off to grieve and attend the funeral, you have to accept that. But she must still make sure that someone is covering for her while she is gone. Her unfortunate circumstances notwithstanding, the cash still needs to be collected and she needs to maintain contact with the office through her Blackberry or cell phone to make sure the business continues to run without her. As the owner, you don't have the same option if you suffer similar bad luck. Payroll needs your final approval even when you are in the midst of an illness or family tragedy.

Excuses are irrelevant to an employee's failure to perform the assigned task. The more you tolerate excuses, the more they arise, and the bigger and more irrelevant they become.

Neither Snow Nor Rain Nor Heat . . .

One of our analysts was caught in a blizzard on his way to a client site in upstate New York. Instead of turning back, he spent the night in his car, risking hypothermia to make sure he could get there on time the following morning. The next time we had an analyst meeting, I presented him with a sleeping bag, so at least he could stay warm and comfortable if he got caught in the next blizzard. Most bosses would have told him not to do that again. That was my way of saying, yes, you had the right attitude. Don't postpone because of the weather. Keep going to the client site. That's the kind of "no excuses" dedication I want to see.

I don't care if there was a traffic jam on the way to work. You've got to enforce the rules. If your business opens at 8 a.m. and employees don't come in until 8.10 a.m., send them home for the day. Shock the crap out of them. When they come back to work the next morning, on time, ask, "Do you get it now?"

The system should always penalize poor or negligent performance. Companies spend too much time worrying about incentives and not enough about penalties.

Sure, give them a couple of chances. Give them a week off without pay as a disciplinary measure. It's legal if they agree to it, and they probably will, because the alternative for them is vacation pay and a pink slip. This tactic can be an effective wake-up call to jolt slacker employees into productivity. But if they still fail, fire 'em sooner rather than later.

As a business owner, you want your people to perform their tasks and fulfill their responsibilities and quotas without question. At the end of the day, it's up to you to put a system in place that enforces discipline. Be personally confrontational with people for not doing what you say. Hold them accountable.

Fear Is the Best Motivator

I was at a client site a couple of years ago, interviewing employees as part of the evaluation process, when one of the workers complained the owner was a total tyrant.

"Bravo," I said. "Then he must be doing something right."

Your business is a place of work, not a country club or a refuge from an unhappy personal life. Make it clear what you expect of your employees, then push and hammer until it gets done. Enforce ironclad discipline. If you don't, watch how the important details get overlooked and the business starts to fail. Fear of not getting a paycheck was, is, and always will be the best motivator.

One of our clients, the owner of a $14 million defense contracting firm in Illinois, had to kick his own son out of the business because he was not performing. The father had previously given him shares in the company, so junior retaliated by getting a $2 million judgment against the business. Meanwhile three top managers—the heads of sales, finance, and operations—threatened to leave the business if the owner didn't give them more authority. And the owner's wife had just been diagnosed with cancer. We call that a bad day.

While all of this was going on, the owner tried to retire. He was losing money, the bank was going to cut his credit line, and three key employees who did all the work were threatening to leave. Clearing our plan with him in advance, we got the CEO and his three managers into a room. We told them they could pick up their checks on Friday if they didn't want to carry out the plan we were about to install. But if they chose to stay, they'd get pay for performance and earn more if our plan was working. The catch was the owner would have to be in control. Of course, the managers stayed. Four years later the owner called us to say he'd sold the business for $15 million. He retired happy and his wife won her battle against cancer.

Of course, I've had clients who've taken this idea that fear is the best motivator philosophy a little too far. A road-paving contractor in Arizona, who shall remain nameless, was in the process of implementing a new work order system with his employees. The CEO called a meeting in the maintenance shop. Before going out to the shop floor he pulled a gun out from under his desk and tucked it into his belt. Then he grabbed a tire iron, explaining, "I never want them to forget who's in charge here."

Forget the firearms. Try to avoid threats of bodily harm. But always remember: YOU are the boss, so act like one. It's not your job to dispense praise, affirmation, hugs, and cookies to your staff. They have to respect you, not like you. Wanting to be liked is perceived as weakness. Your employees will walk all over you. Let them know that you are going to hold them accountable for their actions. Be in control and be controlling. It's better to drive your employees nuts than to lose money.

Don't Let the Inmates Run the Asylum!

Unless, of course, you want to drive yourself crazy and drive the business into a state of total dysfunction and huge losses. I'm not saying you should act like a king. Don't surround yourself with a posse that blows smoke at you. Be a general. You should demand to know everything that's going on in and outside the building. Find out who called, what they said, what the customer wanted, and the best price you can get on those supplies. Breathe down the necks of your workers. Let them know you are watching.

Most problems that occur in my own firm, as well as the others I've worked with, trace back to one fatal characteristic: lack of leadership. You can build confidence in your workforce, and inspire them to do their jobs well, by leading them through down times and presenting yourself as tough, no nonsense, and confident.

It's your business, so you have a right and a responsibility to know everything that's going on. Don't be afraid to ask, "How much does that cost? What are you doing now? Why you are late? Why do you look like you just fell out of bed this morning?" Again, don't tolerate excuses. You have to be insensitive to most problems, unless there is a debilitating illness or death in the family. And by that I don't mean someone's step-uncle's cousin's funeral entitles that person to take a week off.

Don't Just Demand Respect, Command It!

Being a boss doesn't mean you should be above rolling your sleeves up. Good leaders are also role models. You have to be there. You have to let workers know you are in it with them, but they'd better work damn hard when you're not around. If you see trash on the floor, pick it up. It lets people on the floor know that you are not above these menial tasks, and shames them into keeping the place clean and respecting their environment. If a phone on someone's desk rings unanswered, answer it. Workers will see that you consider outside callers, who could be potential customers, to be of utmost priority, and they feel the pressure because their boss is doing their job for them. I do this all the time.

Deserve the respect you demand. Employees should look up to you and follow your orders without a trace of doubt in the back of their minds. Make sure there's a method to your micromanaging madness. You have to have a plan behind the decrees. You can't be a dictator and view yourself as God without a strong operational plan. By all means be tyrannical, but not for its own sake. Be reasonable and clear about the direction you are taking. People accused General George Patton of wanting to be viewed as godlike, but he had a plan to win the battle, and he motivated his men by being at the front of the column. He deserved the respect he commanded.

Fear Is Your Own Best Motivator

Fear shouldn't just motivate your employees. It should motivate you. Never get too comfy. A business owner's internal fear of failure is what keeps the company alive. We just acquired a client—a married couple who own a stationery business—and they are in a state of abject fear. They make about $7 million in sales, but they've lost $1.4 million in four years, and they've maxed out a $1.5 million credit line at the bank. They need to go to their eighty-year-old parents for a loan. They will run out of money in thirty-two days. If they don't fix the business now, they will lose everything. Their terror is palpable. They aren't sleeping. But they're taking ownership of the problem. They're ready to do whatever it takes. Fear has lit a fire under their fannies. They're ready to turn around and be the tough micromanaging bosses they need to be to stem the losses and get the workforce performing again.

Fire Incompetent Employees; They Never Change!

Earlier rather than later.

Getting rid of incompetent workers is probably one of the hardest things bosses have to do. When they sit across the desk from you with their big sad eyes, telling you about the mortgage they're behind on, or the college tuition they have to pay for their kids, it can be gut wrenching. But you have to let the axe fall on deadwood. If you don't, the performers in your business will resent it, and you'll be losing money on payroll for someone who doesn't contribute to the bottom line.

You can't afford to keep them. You don't have those margins for failure. Don't buy the excuses and don't get soft. For the sake of the business, and the hard workers who rely on the business for a living, you should rid yourself of mediocre performers. It's profits in your pocket and lets everyone know you mean business.

Turnover Is a Good Thing . . . Hire Faster

Bread gets stale and milk goes sour. So does an employee's performance. The biggest mistake owners make is trying to rehab employees. Forget it. Identify the prospects who want to perform and can contribute to your bottom line. You may have to hire five to get one, but it's worth it.

Owners agonize for days and weeks over layoffs for any reason. Fire first and agonize later, because every day you wait can cost you hundreds of thousands of dollars in the long run.

This is your opportunity to get out there and find a star performer who can bring up sales or find a hundred little ways to cut costs. Everyone's expendable and there's always someone out there more qualified for a position and more eager for the chance to excel.

We have a client in Queens, New York that makes everything from radiator covers for public schools to finished shower fittings for luxury apartment buildings owned by the likes of Donald Trump. This $6 million business had been in existence for more than sixty years. When the third-generation owner died, his children sold the company to a capable entrepreneur, who saw huge potential in the business despite flat profits.

The new owner, David, is a graduate of Wharton Business School with a strong track record in manufacturing, but he made a huge mistake from the beginning: He didn't fire, or hire, fast enough. He wanted to give the existing employees a chance to prove themselves and allowed his generosity and patience to override his business smarts.

One by one, they took advantage of him. In his first week in charge, more than half the staff disappeared on an extended vacation, claiming they had vacation days to use up. The head of bookkeeping was more interested in where the coffee and rolls came from in the morning than collecting on more than $1 million in unpaid invoices. When another employee left, voluntarily, David discovered the guy had been receiving kickbacks in the form of flat screen TVs and Mets season tickets from a steel supplier, at a cost of 30 percent in inflated materials prices for the business. Several other employees were trading in commodities for the previous owners, during office hours.

Eventually David snapped. But it took more than two years, and a sales manager whose indifference and incompetence lost the company a major contract. We estimate that David lost several hundred thousand dollars due to slow decisions to terminate.

We came in and implemented a spring housecleaning with him. It was easy to sweep out the debris because many employees left of their own accord when they realized they'd be expected to work and be held accountable. Others were fired. Now there are thirty-five employees, and of the twenty original staff members, only two remain. Sales, meanwhile, have more than doubled to $8 million, profit margins are in the healthy double digits, and the company has a huge backlog of contracts despite the fact that the construction business has fallen off a cliff. I rest my case.

Don't put up with mediocrity at any level. Forget sensitivity. Be focused on your plan. If you're a serious business owner you were put here to make money and that's it. Anyone or anything that diminishes your goal must go, and quickly.

Be a tyrant. Graduate from the "Tough Love"
school of management. Your word must be absolute.

∎

Tell your employees: "Don't think, obey."
You want them to do what you say, not what they think.

∎

Brook no deviation; accept no excuses.

∎

It's okay if your employees don't like you, as long as they respect you.
Earn it by getting in the trenches with them.

∎

Remember, fear (of not having a job) is the best motivator.

∎

Don't act like a king; be a general and command the respect you
demand with a clear direction and a precise operational plan.

You Are Not in Business to Pay Your Vendors

HERE'S SOMETHING I'LL BET you haven't read in any other business book: Never pay your bills on time!

You are not in business to pay your vendors. You are in business to make money and build your corporate and personal wealth, using all the resources available to you. Managing a company's outgoing and incoming cash flow is daily hand-to-hand combat. Every day, you're fighting to cover your costs. There never seems to be enough money on hand to make modest capital improvements, pay yourself a reasonable living wage, or cover payroll.

But there is a source of reliable cash, although it's often overlooked and underutilized: *your vendors*. Never paying vendors on time and consciously stretching out your payments to them in an orderly manner is one of your biggest weapons in a constant battle for cash, the life-blood of your business.

Where else is the money going to come from? A weekend in Vegas? Your maxed-out line of credit at the bank? Maxed-out credit cards? You cannot count on getting cash from these sources when you need it most. Cash management is always the toughest problem for most business owners.

Think of every dollar you can defer paying as an interest-free loan. If you are struggling, paying your invoices on time gets you nowhere. Paying your bills one day faster than you have to is throwing cash away. The only people you will be making happy are your vendors. Why not keep the cash instead?

Stall to Survive

Stop worrying about your credit rating and start worrying about your cash on hand. You can't kill yourself to pay your bills on time. You have to focus on having enough cash to survive and build your business.

Instead of stressing over writing checks to your vendors, you should view them as your best source of financing. Use their money aggressively. If you have $50,000 or $500,000 in bills, can gain an extra thirty days on the whole amount, and keep this amount outstanding at the same level, you have just given yourself a $50,000 to $500,000 permanent interest-free loan. Every dollar deferred is as an expansion of free credit.

If I had suggested to my finance professors that you should do everything you can not to pay your bills and stretch your credit, I'm not sure whether they would have given me an A or an F and kicked me out of class. This isn't what Harvard Business School teaches you. You won't find a how-to guide that advises you to use and abuse your vendors as much as you can, albeit legally and politely.

According to conventional wisdom, what I am saying is a sacrilege.

The "experts" would advise you pay your bills on time to get more credit. Frankly, this is good advice if you have a surplus of cash. But if your business is failing, you have to determine whether you would rather delay payment or keep your credit rating, run out of cash, and cease operations. The choice is obvious: You can take a salary cut, lose money for lack of supplies, and fail to cover your children's school bills, or you can run your business and live a good life by expanding your cash inflow.

Not paying your bills on time may be a new way of thinking to many of you. But this is an important, extreme, and real world business survival tactic that most successful business owners will tell you they have used to survive at one point in their careers.

You should not lie. That's wrong. But being evasive and noncommittal about your next payment is not. It's okay to say, "Call me back in a few days." Just make sure you take the call. It's a good business survival tactic, and one that the real winners practice all the time.

All you have to do is pick up the phone and start negotiating on an honest, realistic basis with your vendors. If someone is giving you 30-day terms, go back to them and ask them for 60-day terms, then pay them a few days late. If you negotiate with your vendors, you can always buy a few more days, and you might be surprised at better terms than that. Remember, in most cases they need your business as much as you need the business of your clients. Besides, vendors are probably better financed than you are, and can afford the slow payment.

It's in the Mail

The same rule applies to rent. Don't rush to pay your landlord. Sit with him or her and explain that you need at least thirty days more to pay up. You can also negotiate the total amount and timing of rent payments to lower them and stagger them farther apart. In most cases the landlord is not going to throw you out, and needs you in that space more than ever.

You may not be a big guy to the landlord, but you are still important. The cost of getting a new tenant, if your landlord can find one, is way beyond the cost of evicting you. Obviously, you should take the time to deliver the message. And expect some resistance. Many landlords will say they have to pay the mortgage on the first of the month, but that's not your problem. Just be careful not to break down the relationship.

Be realistic. When you expand your payables, don't do it by ducking calls and hiding from the people trying to collect. Don't ruin your relationships and have them not ship to you. Communicate what you are doing. Act like a diplomat and just keep talking. Tell them when you plan on paying them, and then do your best to honor your word. If you can't pay as you renegotiated, try paying something, as a show of good will. Then give them an indication that they will get their full payment eventually. This tactic buys you more time. They might kick and scream, but they would rather know they can count on that money coming in ninety days than never.

An easy way to keep the cash is to stop using outside payroll services. The big banks and payroll services have bamboozled small and midsized businesses for many years. They make you fund your payroll two or three days before it's even due, so they can play the float (the outstanding check amount that has not yet cleared the bank), and maximize their own profits, not yours. If your payroll is Friday, for example, you have to pre-fund that payment, along with the appropriate taxes, on Wednesday. Many of the paychecks would not clear until the following week. By eliminating prepaid bank checks, and including the two or three days it takes a paycheck to clear, you will have gained a week of float—$10,000, $25,000, or $100,000—depending on the payroll. This money will become a permanent interest-free loan. Most payroll services will let you use your regular checks, but they never tell you about that option unless you ask. This lack of disclosure is not illegal, but certainly deceptive. But if you don't ask, it's your fault! You are allowing the bank the use of YOUR money for a week, permanently, with no interest!

Like the banks, many large corporations are equally, and legally, ruthless in the way they save and accumulate cash flow at the expense of their customers and clients. Some major retailers have been known to damage at least one pallet when they receive a shipment. That way, they can take the goods but leave something on the loading dock. When the vendor sends in the invoice and follows up thirty days later asking where the money is, the big box customer can then say, "You have to pick up your damaged goods first, and then send us an adjusted invoice." It stalls payment by at least a couple more months.

That just shows how tough-minded big business can be when it comes to cash. Large companies employ people to figure out ways to hold onto their cash. When they're short of money they start paying later. Why not follow suit? You don't have to pull dirty tricks to get the same result.

Keep a list of A-list, B-list, and C-list vendors. Your A-list vendors are the ones you can't afford to lose. Business depends on getting their shipments on time. So pay them at the end of 30 days, or 35 if you can, and pay the B-list vendors in 60 days, and the C-listers in 90 days. If they protest, pay them in 65 days, or 95 days, then go back to 60 and 90 the next billing cycle, to keep them happy. Believe me, it will.

If you get badly overdue, make sure when paying your bills that the money you've sent applies to the oldest balance, and, wherever possible, never pay extra on the old balance for new orders. If, for example, you have just ordered $10,000 of goods, and owe $50,000 in outstanding payables, don't pay more than the $10,000 for the goods that you receive. The vendor will pressure you for the full amount up front, but don't cave in. Otherwise you would be contracting your balance, which takes assets (in the form of cash) out of your business.

Never pay late fees, and never pay down your balance. Forget about your credit rating and survive.

Cash Flow Is King

When we arrive at companies with major problems paying their bills, our first step is to discuss the current situation with the companies' vendors. The business owners usually have lost all credibility, and we become the lightning rod for the vendors to vent. We get an earful about their general displeasure with our clients' lack of payment and missed promises in the past.

We worked with an electrical contractor client in West Virginia four years ago who was deader than dead. It was the usual story that leads up to that point: zero materials and cost controls in place and nonexistent financial management. They hired us as a last resort. It was either that or shutter the business altogether.

We notified every vendor to let them know we were restructuring the company's list of payables, and that they would be getting a payoff plan within a few days. Then we notified the bank and met with the loan officers and manager in person. Neither the bank nor the vendors believed for a second that we would be able to get our hands on cash from the business and get things under control. One loan officer even laughed. But we were serious. NO vendors got paid for thirty days. Most of them were cooperative and worked with us. In most cases, they were giving discounts. It gave us just enough room to turn things around. Within eighteen months the bank debt, which exceeded $1 million, had been paid in full. The loan officer who found the situation amusing said:

"You guys must be magicians, because I have never seen anything like that before. I'd have written off that business long ago!"

But if we had not dealt with the vendors and squeezed out some cash from the situation first, that business would not have survived three more months. Stalling payments is a move that makes the difference between the life and death of a business.

Remember the exotic pet store owner in Virginia from Chapter 6? He was at the end of the line. But by negotiating with his landlord, we saved him $25,000 a month for three months. That $75,000 gave him the cash to keep the lights on and got him the time he needed to expand his payables, cut costs, fire unnecessary staff, and stave off foreclosure until the next sales cycle in the spring.

It's Never Over 'Til It's Over

The constant stress of a cash shortage would make any of us myopic and unable to see a way out. Stressed-out owners have been doing a dance for so long with the bill collectors they become overwhelmed and try to hide from the problems. A bunker mentality overcomes them.

We had one client, the owner of a $9 million pump manufacturer in Tennessee, who swore to us he'd done everything he could to expand his credit and payables. He told us he'd been trying for months with the unions, the workers, the bank, the vendors, and the IRS. No one would give him an inch. It was hooey. As is so often the case, the answer was just a phone call away. As a third party, we got him reductions to the tune of $400,000 in one day. It was just a question of helping his vendors see it would be in their best interests to give the guy a break.

Many business owners in this situation borrow their way into a deeper hole to make the nasty phone calls stop. With declining sales and losses, borrowing more only amplifies the cash problem. Many times owners have already capped their home equity and credit cards, and may be overwhelmed by personal lawsuits and foreclosure.

Two years ago we worked with two brothers who owned a small chain of diners down South. They ran their business and personal lives on the "float." First it was $30,000, then it was $50,000, and soon they were overdrawn more than $200,000. Every time they felt pressure from a vendor they'd pull their checkbook out and write the check. They had no idea what checks and total amounts they had outstanding, and couldn't therefore determine how much money they needed to cover the float. Many checks were bouncing daily. The bank was furious, and the company was paying $3,000 a week in extra bank charges. It was a mess. They should have tackled the problem head-on and bought time with the vendors instead of paying them off with rubber checks and wiping out any trust they had left.

Be Honest, Be Nice, and Be Late

Your money flow doesn't just dry up by itself. An accumulation of losses, cash leaks, and lousy sales, along with financial mismanagement, create the problem. Whatever the reason, and whoever is at fault, you don't have to stand with your back against the wall. Vendors will keep trying to take a bite out of you until you say, "Stop! Things aren't working well now. You are just going to have to calm down and wait until I get a recovery plan in place."

When you reach this point, it requires drastic action. If your overall cash strategy doesn't change NOW, no amount of negotiating and fast talking with collectors, vendors, or banks will prevent your business from failing. Expanding your payables, in an orderly fashion, must be a part of any plan to maintain cash flow. It is especially important in businesses with significant sales declines, bank credit problems, and overdue payables.

Take the necessary steps today to establish a realistic, tough cash flow plan. Implement that plan without conscience, and you will find enough peace of mind to work at reestablishing profitability.

Vendors say you are their most valued customer, but that's a load of horse manure. They don't care about you. Pay late and hold onto your money. It's ruthless, but it's good business practice in any economy.

You might not make your vendors' holiday card list, but so what? At least you'll have enough cash flow to help your business survive and thrive. Cash is only king when you have it and they don't. When times are tough and you don't have the money to cover your taxes or payroll, you need to have an iron rod up your spine. It might get ugly, but *financial failure is not an option.*

Remember: There's always one last financial trick in your bag that can save you . . .

You Are Not in Business to Pay Your Vendors

Never pay your vendors on time.

■

Stretch out payments from thirty days to sixty days and ninety days,
and then pay a few days late again.

■

Your vendors are your best source of interest-free financing.
Use them aggressively.

■

Keep a list of A-list, B-list, and C-list vendors. The most important
suppliers and service providers get paid first, but still late.

■

Be honest and fair. Don't duck calls. Be a diplomat: get on
the phone to stall and negotiate, politely. You'll be surprised
what you can get out of them, especially in a recession.

■

Same goes for rent. You won't get evicted if you're thirty days late.
Your landlord needs to keep you as a tenant just as much as
your business needs its four walls.

When Filing for Bankruptcy Is Your Best Option, Do It Early!

CHAPTER 11 REORGANIZATION, COMMONLY known as bankruptcy, allows you to barely pay your vendors at all. It erases 80 percent to 90 percent of your debt, prevents your bank from foreclosing your loans, allows you to eliminate leases and contracts that you don't like, and rebuilds your equity, cash flow, and profits. All litigation against your company stops, and no one is allowed to ask for past due money without court approval.

So why wouldn't I recommend this step as a fabulous legal financial maneuver? I do recommend it, at the right time and the right place, and urge you to file more often, and much earlier, than the actual current practice.

Be warned. This remedy takes a strong stomach. You'll need the ability to withstand massive pressure from lifelong friends, your community, family members, and employees, and maintain an unwavering commitment to your self-preservation and profits.

It's a devastating choice to have to make, and the social stigma of filing for Chapter 11 often prevents business owners from taking this important and necessary step. They are waiting for their next big contract, expansion of their line of credit, or a private investor. They mistakenly believe the bank won't foreclose on them, the IRS won't seize their assets, and their creditors will stop suing or hounding them for payments. The next thing that happens is usually all of the above. The business fails, and you are looking at starting the rest of your life with nothing.

But if you file for Chapter 11 Reorganization early enough, before your assets and cash flow run out and it becomes an act of sheer desperation, you will have a much better chance of achieving a successful bankruptcy. You will stay in business for many months and years as you rebuild profits and, most important, your own compensation.

When to File?

You are eligible to file if your company's assets (at market value) are worth less than your liabilities, or you are unable to pay your bills when they come due. That's when you are able to seek bankruptcy protection from the court.

A classic example of a well-timed bankruptcy is Dow Corning. The company filed a Chapter 11 while it was making millions of dollars, but had built up huge potential liabilities over its manufacturing of defective breast implants, which were having devastating effects on patients. Dow Corning could not have paid all those potential lawsuits had they come due. The company averted failure by filing a Chapter 11, making a settlement on the lawsuits, and emerging as a big ongoing corporate enterprise.

Delta Airlines also completed a reorganization from which it has emerged stronger than before, delivering a $3 billion boost to their balance sheet and operating profits. The company used reorganization under the strict rules of the court to transform its business, and exited bankruptcy a year earlier than planned.

Success stories notwithstanding, most business owners overlook the intent of the law, which is to allow a failing company, whatever the reasons for its demise, to rebuild and reorganize while freezing all financial pressure in place. If you have $500,000 of corporate debt, for example, it's likely you can settle these bills for $50,000 paid out over three to five years. If it's $5 million, the same percentages apply. If you owe the IRS a small or large amount of money, the law also provides shelter, time, and compromise on your debt. All leases and contracts can be broken with the court's approval, even current leases for real estate and contracts for inventory. You can work out new financial arrangements on these items going forward or abandon the contracts.

Many business owners don't understand the law, which is made mystical by some of the less scrupulous bankruptcy lawyers. Lawyers too often try to control the business aspects of the company rather than explain options clearly to their clients. Of course there are all levels of bankruptcy lawyers, but some are as predatory as vultures preying on the carcass of a dying small business. If they don't like my saying it, sue me!

The law is not that complicated. Today when you file, most of your financial obligations are suspended in time and can only be enforced by a judicial court order. As the "debtor in possession," you can remain in control of the operations of your business, subject to oversight and jurisdiction of the court. You can use incoming cash from many of your normal sources to pay current bills, and cannot by law pay any old bills due previous to the date of filing.

Sounds like an interesting solution to an overwhelming debt load, doesn't it?

Frankly, it is. And it's completely legal. The obvious downfall is that a judge controls everything from your salary to how you spend your cash. You have to follow the rules of the court regarding current expenses. And then there is the additional fallout: some angry creditors (in the short term), potential loss of business, serious pangs of conscience over not paying your bills, as well as the general humiliation of perceived defeat.

Many argue against Chapter 11 Reorganization: The lawyers cost too much; you will lose sales because of the stigma; your company won't snap back as fast as you might hope, and you can accomplish the same results of a Chapter 11 filing through what these critics call an "informal bankruptcy." These are all legitimate arguments, but they pale against the huge benefits achieved with a formal reorganization.

Life's winners make the tough decision to file. Those who don't can always say they tried to pay all their bills. Unfortunately, trying to cover all of your payables usually leaves you and your family without a dime. You are left with the ensuing problems of no income and financial failure, which will probably follow you for years. This is the time to forget your social conscience and put you and your family first. *The Tough Choice is the Right Choice!*

A Tale of Two Companies

We have spent time with many clients who are in Chapter 11, or are close to becoming another bankruptcy statistic. Here are two examples and their surprising outcomes:

The first business was an $11 million automotive parts distributor and retailer in Motor City (we have a lot of these; they represent a sizeable chunk of America's economy). Over the last three years, sales dropped to $4.5 million, and they were operating on losses in the hundreds of thousands in an industry racked with problems and plummeting sales. This business owed the IRS $100,000 in unpaid payroll taxes. Because of its straight-line decline in sales and profits, their bank yanked the company's $1 million line of credit.

The second business, located in Northern Minnesota, was a kitchen installation contractor and made $47 million in sales at its peak in 2005. Last year, sales dropped to $500,000 a month, or a mere $6 million a year. The company owed millions of dollars to its bank, and millions more to leasing companies and suppliers, as well as hefty taxes to the IRS.

These were barely functioning companies on the edge of survival. So what did they do?

The automotive business resisted Chapter 11. The stamp of failure through declaring bankruptcy was so daunting they decided not to proceed. No one can blame them. They wanted to go out with their heads held high. They cut their salaries to $48,000 from $150,000, mortgaged their homes, cashed out their 401(k)s, and tapped family assets, including their elderly parents' estate, to pay off the $1 million to the bank. Now they have nothing. The former partners are facing divorce from their spouses. They can't support their families and they can't come up with tuition for their college-bound kids. Their personal assets are depleted and they are flat broke. But, hey, at least they didn't declare bankruptcy!

The second business, the kitchen contractor, filed Chapter 11. They reorganized, with a court-supervised plan that reduced their debt to vendors by 95 percent, paid out over five years. The banks were forced by the judge to take back all unused equipment, valued in the millions, and cancel that debt when these assets were returned. The IRS settled with the company and agreed to a five-year payment plan. The bank's line of credit was reduced to a manageable amount. The company has restored a modest level of profitability to the same level of sales—still about $6 million a year. Now it has the breathing room to rebuild.

The business that had the farthest to fall fared better than the one that resisted bankruptcy. A lot better. This contractor still has a pulse, and it's looking more and more like it's going to stay alive. Without the label of Chapter 11, anyone would say it performed a neat legal and financial manipulation to save itself.

Timing Is Everything

We tried to help an electrical contractor in Kentucky save itself with a Chapter 11 filing. Let's call it "OntheWire, Inc." This company was in business for over thirty years, but after averaging about $5 million a year, sales dropped to just over $3 million a year. The company owed millions. The owner had a country club membership, a $1.2 million primary mortgage, a second home with a $400,000 mortgage, a loan for a $100,000 boat . . . you get the idea. He also owes the IRS $350,000 in arrears, and $80,000 in state taxes.

OntheWire continues to operate. The owner is taking as much cash out of the business as he can. He's getting up at 6 a.m., six days a week and insists he's getting new business, but it's getting more and more difficult to sustain day-to-day operations. He's selling off trucks and equipment to try to raise cash, but at rock-bottom prices. He refused to restructure, and he's on deathwatch now. A strict, court-enforced reorganization could have saved him, but in his mind that would have been worse than certain corporate demise.

I'm not saying it should be a troubled company's first option. There is a time and place for filing for court-supervised reorganization. Chapter 11 is a great financial mechanism if you want to save your business. But don't forget: do it earlier rather than later.

I am not passing judgment on the morality or ethics of this choice. Congress put these laws in place for a reason. It remains the only legitimate way to defeat a tsunami of debt. And thousands upon thousands of companies have taken advantage of the bankruptcy reorganization act in a tough, disciplined fashion to survive.

Survival First

I've seen good people resist bankruptcy because either they believe the next contract is almost at their doorstep, or they can't live with the idea that their vendors won't get paid. They think the vendors are their friends and they don't want to hurt them because they've had a relationship for years. But when it comes down to dollars, if it's their money, the vendors, the bank, the IRS, the suppliers, and the clients, will put themselves first. Many small business owners on the edge cling to the belief that their vendors will work with them and give them a break. But these companies no longer exist because they had their assets liquidated by their "friends" at the bank.

I understand how hard it is. Everybody titters when they hear you are in bankruptcy. There's a widespread cynicism about Chapter 11. People believe you're trying to pull a fast one. But I have never seen small business owners take this step lightly. When they reach this point, they are in dire straits. Their only mistake is not having done it sooner.

When I first started in this business, I spent a lot of time standing right beside my clients in bankruptcy court. Many of these men and women were distraught. Some even wept. Several said it felt like a death in the family. It's a rough, nasty, emotional up and down. The family is confused. Creditors get vicious. There is an overwhelming feeling of failure, and the time leading up to the day in bankruptcy court can be sheer torture.

But the day after, it's as if a huge anvil has lifted from the owner's shoulders and the business can start to move forward. There's a sense of renewed energy in the company. If the situation is explained to employees correctly, there's also a sense of excitement and urgency about the prospects of the business.

Stand Tall

Some people see this move as immoral or shameful, but I commend these business owners for making it when they did. They had the guts and commitment to make their businesses work.

I hope you never have to face this dilemma. If you can implement some or all of the Profit Rules, you won't have to take this step. But none of us is perfect and if, like thousands of other small business owners, you are faced with this choice, you're not alone . . . Chapter 11 can be a tremendous benefit to your business. It allows you to erase the largest part of your mistakes and renew your business track to profits and success.

When Filing for Bankruptcy Is Your Best Option, Do It Early!

Timing is everything in a successful Chapter 11 Reorganization.

■

Make sure you have enough assets and sources of income left
to survive and rebuild your business.

■

Get over the shame of it and put survival first.

■

See Chapter 11 for what it is: a legal and financial maneuver
that will help you deal with a tsunami of debt.

■

Don't let the bankruptcy lawyers mystify you.
The law is not that complicated. It freezes most of your debt in place
and gives you the breathing room to rebuild.

■

Chapter 11 takes time, hard work, and sacrifice,
but you'll come out stronger.

Don't Treat Sales
Like Your Mother-in-Law

JUST LIKE YOUR SALES effort, you know you have to put up with her, but you'd rather not. You're unhappy when she comes, you got along fine without her, and you're thrilled when she leaves.

The same goes for sales. As far as you're concerned, your sales team just gets in the way when they're around. They're an afterthought. You believe if you have the right product, it will sell, because somehow you are the chosen one. God forbid you should have to get your hands dirty and go out there yourself. There is something a little distasteful about having to get out from behind your desk, roll your sleeves up, and shill.

Get Over It!

If sales are down, there's always something, or someone else to blame: incompetent sales staff, a declining economy, an ever-shrinking niche market, the government, and politicians. Yes, these factors have an impact on everyone's sales levels, but if you're losing sales and heading for financial trouble, it's your fault.

Large or small, if your business doesn't have a disciplined, aggressive, and accountable sales program, it will fail. And that's exactly what's happening to thousands of small businesses, where making sales requires constant, disciplined effort.

You are only as good as your sales personnel. Most business owners don't have a clue how to conceive and construct a disciplined sales effort. Many have engineering backgrounds, and prefer to stay inside their comfort zone on the operations side of the business. Others are second- and third-generation owners and have lived too long off the net worth of the business they inherited. Still others possess an inflated view of how important their business is to the marketplace. But underneath the bravado they live in quiet fear of failure. They are terrified of rejection by prospective clients. Throw into this schizophrenic mix a general contempt for sales staff.

But by far the biggest crime against sales is the owner's unwillingness to mix it up with customers. Retailers and restaurateurs are among the worst culprits. They expect customers to walk through the door with next to no external marketing, and blame landlords and mall owners when there's no traffic. They refuse to be out front in the sales effort. They prefer to work the "back of the house" and allow poorly paid underlings to handle customer service in the dining area. Meanwhile, they give their maitre d's and waitstaff no incentive to ensure that diners keep coming back.

Larger enterprises are just as guilty. Owners don't attend regular sales meetings, never look at daily sales reports, and barely go on customer calls because "they're too busy." They avoid installing telemarketing programs and telemarketing personnel, because they don't like to take calls themselves. They don't pay for performance and accept it when a mediocre salesperson says, "I am trying just as hard on salary as I would be on commission." This last one is ludicrous. Clearly if you need sales for your paycheck, you'll try harder. Remember pay for performance?

I'm afraid there's just no way around this one. If you don't have your sales strategy down pat, if you haven't built a disciplined sales team with telemarketing, customer support, and regular reports that you look at every day, then you aren't covering even the basics of your business. If you are abdicating and allowing your inadequate sales team to BS you because you just don't want to deal with it yourself, you are neglecting the single most effective way to drive profit growth. If you turn your back on your mother-in-law, she'll have the ultimate revenge because you are going to fail.

Making your sales effort stronger is the easy answer and the one profit strategy that works. You have got to do the basics for the market you are in.

Fat, Dumb, and Happy

As I said from the beginning, this book is intended to instill a change in attitude. I'm not going to waste words giving you a long "how-to" checklist for sales. There are plenty of books out there for that. The problem is that you aren't doing it and you aren't taking the initiative to read about it. Read and study those books. A boom-time economy has made most small business owners dangerously complacent. They were making an adequate living working fewer hours and most years ended up with increased sales and sometimes profits.

I came across a classic example of this kind of apathy not long ago, when I was helping two partners in a pricey jewelry store. These women started their business a few years ago and couldn't keep their hot-selling items in stock. They asked for my help because their sales had plummeted over 50 percent. The first thing I noticed was they weren't keeping track of their customers' names, addresses, and emails. If they had done this over the past five years, they would have several thousand email addresses to use as a marketing tool. They could be in constant contact with their past customers to promote trunk sales, wine and cheese tastings, or Monday night discounts. It was a surefire way of generating new sales traffic.

Simple enough, right?

Except that two months later, the two women still hadn't taken my advice. During that time they could have collected two or three hundred names. Instead, they chose to cut their own salaries. When I asked them why they failed to implement even the most rudimentary customer outreach program, they said didn't like receiving mass emails and knew their customers felt the same way. They were too embarrassed to collect names and blast out the occasional sales flyer, for fear people would be annoyed by the extra spam in their in-boxes.

These are two charming and classy women. They have a beautiful store. Sadly, they'll probably be out of business in six months, as soon as their lease is up.

Wrap Your Customers in a Warm and Fuzzy Cocoon

Don't be like the jewelry store owners. Don't allow yourself and your staff to let people just walk in and walk out. You've got to build an information base and reach out. Businesses like shops and restaurants have plenty of downtime to write and edit email blasts, and could find lots of creative and unobtrusive ways to collect contact details from customer traffic.

When I walk along the streets, I see so many vacant premises that once belonged to restaurants and stores. They're dropping like flies, and it shouldn't be that way. It's easy to blame the economy but the underlying cause is the business owner's unwillingness to do the obvious: get out there and hustle.

Business owners can't afford the luxury of sitting back. We're working with a contractor now who makes granite countertops. He received fifteen orders a week from Lowe's. By the time we got there, he was lucky if he got one a month. Sales were down 80 percent. He should have been going out there finding other customers before the tide turned. Now he's being forced to learn sales strategies from scratch as his business hangs on the line. He has no idea how and it's a tough road ahead.

But if you're proactive about sales and pay a little more attention to your sales effort before it wreaks havoc, there are plenty of things you can do to generate customer sales.

Get Focused!

Car dealerships are failing by the hundreds each month, and most owners are blaming the economy and the problems of GM, Chrysler, and Ford. I do not agree. The desperate straits they find themselves in are largely self-inflicted.

We asked one automotive supplier outside Detroit how much business came from the car companies. The owner assumed that 60 percent of his business came from the Big Three when in fact, after looking at his books, it was 80 percent. The fate of his business was in their hands.

He could have installed an aggressive sales force while he had the cash flow, but he assumed the easy money would always be there. He never believed these huge companies that gave him business would fail. As the industry crashed through the floor, his sales fell from $10 million to $6 million. He didn't build up his sales capabilities in good times so it wouldn't go south in bad times. He was operating under the misconception that the good years will carry you through.

It's not too late. His business still has a pulse, and it might survive if the owner gets aggressive about building a well-tuned and well-motivated sales department. But now he's just scrambling for business with no direction or game plan.

There are many creative ways for car dealers to survive. Don't assume all new sales are going to come through the main door. A lot of business can be generated out of the side doors and back doors. We worked with a Buick dealership in Iowa that started building out sales from its service department. Most dealers don't assume that everyone coming to get their car serviced would also buy a new car from them, and they do nothing to try to bring these customers back. But at this dealership, any kind of traffic was treated as a potential customer. It also drove up service department revenue through extra line items such as headlight bulbs or new windshield wipers for every new repair order, and gave the service staff incentives for making those sales. The dollar amounts were small, but they added up.

The dealership didn't stop there. It expanded its hours, and started attacking its sales on the front end by calling old customers and building a list of customer referrals. Every day the sales staff made sure they made several sales calls. It even started advertising locally with posters and banners and soon became one of the top five Buick dealerships in the country.

You're Not Dead Yet

You simply can't afford to be passive anymore. Not that you ever could. In boom-times and bad, you owe it to yourself and your business to be out there fighting for every dollar. You might be telling yourself there's nothing you can do about it so you can hang back and wait until the bad times pass. If that's your attitude, go and shoot yourself. Close your business and find another job.

The market's never dead. There's always business to be found, if you're looking hard enough. People will always need goods and services. As your competitors go out of business, you can pick up their best customers if you're smart and aggressive about it. If you'd been doing what you were supposed to all along, you'd already be replacing lost customers with new ones.

If You Build It . . .

A few months ago Lou Mosca was inspired by an email alert from *Crain's New York Business* that had the latest commercial construction statistics in the metro area. The report estimated business was at $41 billion in 2008, and slid to $29 billion. Lou said to himself, "Yeah, the pool has shrunk, but $29 billion is still a damn big pool!" He realized that the better subcontracting companies needed to get aggressive and fight for whatever business was left in the pot.

Lou met with several of our sub-contractor clients in the metro New York area. Dozens of them, who previously had revenues of $5 million to $50 million, were experiencing sales drops of more than 50 percent. They had almost no backlog, and no idea where the new contracts were going to come from. Lou went over their sales processes with them. We even offered to send in one of our sales consultants for a day or two, for free, to help them to come up with a plan on bidding for work from architects and engineers. But these guys just weren't interested. They told Lou they had been doing it the same way for twenty-five years and that business would come back, they just had to hang on.

It was a twisted logic Lou couldn't deal with. Until recently, most subcontractors assumed business would come to them from general contractors. They'd wait for their names to appear on the bid, or read the *Dodge Bulletin*, an industry report, to see what opportunities were coming up. But God forbid they should go out and find new business on their own.

Lou got through to a few of our clients. In fact, we just launched a new sales program for a subcontractor in South Carolina who installs heating, ventilation, and air conditioning systems into buildings. Initially, he only took jobs within his own county. But, one by one, his usual customers disappeared. The subcontractor realized he had to expand his sales footprint because it was either that or certain bankruptcy.

Live It

Live and breathe sales daily. It's not just enough to hire good and aggressive salespeople with strong track records. It is your job to be out in front of your sales troops and making some of those sales calls yourself. You need to establish personal relationships with your sales force as well as your customers.

Know your customers intimately so you are never beholden to your sales reps. We worked with a $16 million printing company eight years ago in Delaware that had been losing money for two years. The partners weren't focused on sales, and 90 percent of their customers' communication was with the inside sales support staff. Within two months of making the owners go on sales calls with their field reps and meeting with people in person, they were profitable.

After we left the project, the owners slipped back into their lazy ways. They let their sales reps in the field handle everything. They never talked to their customers directly. Even the biggest clients couldn't get the owners on the phone. When two sales reps left they took their customers with them, and sales dropped 50 percent. Within a year the company went bankrupt.

Yes, You Can!

We've seen so many businesses fall like leaves off a tree lately. Even big companies like Circuit City haven't been immune to the lousy market. Circuit City senior management now admits that their decision to fire their better paid and more successful sales staff can be attributed to the failure of the company. But that doesn't have to be your fate if you have the guts and fortitude get busy with sales now.

We worked with a truck distributor outside of Minneapolis who was in serious trouble after losing one of his biggest clients. Most of his business came from the municipalities. When their budgets were slashed it looked like his business would die.

Lou took the owner, along with his sales staff, and locked them in a hotel room with him for the day (on a Saturday). Together, they hammered out specific sales goals, timelines, and ways to achieve sales targets. The owner changed his business model, expanding his sales to the entire Midwest and adding new items such as trailers and snowplows that could be sold to captive markets like school districts. Profits have been high every year since.

I don't care how bad things look. Get up off your chair and get busy. You can do it.

Don't Treat Sales Like Your Mother-in-Law

Don't view sales like an unwanted guest. Focusing on sales
is the easiest way to grow your business in good times
and sustain it in bad times.

■

Get out from behind your desk, roll up your sleeves, and shill!

■

Collect names and build a database of customers.

■

Expand your geographical footprint and diversify so you're not
dependent on one big company for the bulk of business.

■

Breathe down the necks of your sales team.
Go on sales calls with them. If they're not performing, fire 'em.

■

Wrap your clients in a warm and fuzzy cocoon. If you don't, and your
top sales guy leaves and takes your customers with him, shame on you!

■

Stop being "fat, dumb, and happy." Get lean and hungry.
It's time to fight for every last dollar!

Give Up Golf, Retreats, Off-Sites, and Trade Shows

ARE YOU LOOKING FOR a great way to fritter away time you could be spending on bringing in more business?

I suggest golf.

Yes, I'm serious. It's a waste of time. And so are office seminars, frivolous conventions, and "planning retreats." And while I'm at it, dump the trade shows! They're just a flimsy excuse for a paid vacation.

There is no justification for doing anything other than work during office hours. Oh sure, you can call it "networking" when you play golf or go to a seminar; you can tell yourself the mountain retreat is motivating your employees; you can kid yourself that your entire staff needs to be at the trade convention, manning the booth or searching for new product lines. But be honest. How many business deals get done at these things? How long before the feel-good factor of that office volleyball game fades? A week? Do you really think playing golf with your bank manager is going to guarantee you a loan? And the last time I checked, nobody made money off of trade shows. Trade shows attract shoppers, not buyers. If you miss a product launch, so what? The same sales reps who were at the Javitz Center in New York City will be on the road for the next three months showing off their new wares to anyone who will take a sales call. Why go to them when you know they'll come to you?

Birdies, Bogies, and Bankruptcy

Most of the business owners I've dealt with over the years love to hit the fairway. There's just something about donning those plaid pants and driving those little carts that invigorates the ego and makes people feel like they belong to a special class of fat cats. They tell themselves they have to be out there. They're schmoozing for business and honing their reputations with the rest of the big players. But when you're running a small business, how much time can you afford to spend away from the office? It's time and money you should be putting into your business.

Look at it this way. If you joined a place like the Bay Hill Country Club in Orlando at, say, a $25,000 initiative fee, and became a member for twenty years at $5,000 in annual club dues and $150 for green fees, you'd be out $300,000. Do you expect to reap that much in profits from frolicking on the grass? And I'm not factoring in the price of all the post-game Scotches and the opportunities you missed while you were on the links instead of working the phones to drum up new business.

And yet, well over half of our clients are addicted to golf. They knock off work early and play tournaments in the middle of the week. Maybe if you're golfing with Bill Gates, there's something in it for you, but unless someone of that caliber wants to be your fairway friend, don't bother. Most of the time you'll find yourself putting alongside your bank manager or loan officer. Believe me, they'll almost always accept an invitation to midweek tee off times. They've got nothing to lose. It's not their payroll. If anything, they're looking to cash in on what they can get out of you! The bank pays their salary either way. But if you don't qualify for a bigger credit line, those nine holes aren't going to help.

Last year I was at a Partner America golf event for mayors and business owners in Augusta, Georgia, home of the annual Masters Tournament. Before the tournament I was doing a seminar, and I thought it was going well, until I told the audience to give up golf. I almost got booed and hissed out of the room, until I asked the jeering golf lovers in the crowd how many $100,000 deals they made while playing eighteen holes. No hands went up. Again, I asked, when a little two-hour round turns into six, followed by a nice glass of Scotch in the clubhouse afterwards, how many important phone calls did they miss? There was silence.

Okay, maybe I was killing the mood, but for good reason. Sure, it's important to get out there once in a while, but when you're building a business and trying to get it to a point where it's self-sustaining, there are more important tasks in front of you than there are on the back nine. Golf isn't even good exercise!

By all means go to Myrtle Beach once a year for a week to play golf with your buddies. Clear your head. I understand the appeal of an environment with no cell phones or Blackberries. But if you need that extra head space, you'd be better off following the example of one of my favorite clients, whom we'll call "Lenny."

Lenny joined his local country club, but not to play golf. He hated the game, considering it a waste of time. He'd use the clubhouse for a social lunch or dinner, and some quiet time away from the office to reflect, but never for more than an hour.

"George, I'd rather be out there chasing the dollars than spending five hours chasing some stupid ball," he told me.

Seven years ago, Lenny was making $24 million, and now he makes $60 million, all because he concentrated his efforts on making the most of his networking time instead of wasting hours knocking around a little ball just to lead up to it. He had his priorities right.

Drastic and Iconoclastic

Lou hates the game. He sees it as an elitist hobby for snobs and social-ites. That's because Lou's a down-to-earth, roll-up-your-sleeves, and get-to-work kind of guy who'd rather see a Mets game . . . but in his spare time, of course. Some of his biggest arguments have been with bull-headed clients who are avid golfers.

He is so adamant about this belief that he clashed with the owner of an office supply company in central New Jersey that sold fax machines and copiers. Let's call him Bill Schwartz. Big box stores like Office Depot and Staples, as well as online competition, were squeezing his company's profit margins, and Lou was giving the management some of his usual tough love, with detailed suggestions for cutting costs and improving systems from top to bottom.

But the owner had different ideas. He didn't see himself as the prob-lem. He blamed his service department, and the thirty other employees he was supposed to be leading. He ordered Lou to meet with them one by one. But Lou thought this process would be pointless. He knew this CEO wasn't as interested in doing what was right for the business. He was more interested in showing that he was the big boss.

They ended up in a screaming match. Well . . . not exactly. It was one-sided. Lou stayed calm, but this guy was livid. He told Lou, "I've been in business here for years, and I know what I'm doing. I'm a pillar of this community. You don't tell me what to do!"

"Fine, Mr. Schwartz," replied Lou. "But that's not what the numbers say. If you're doing so well, why don't you prove it to me?"

He made Lou get in his car—a showy two-seater Mercedes convertible—and drove Lou to his house. Lou was supposed to be impressed. It was a palatial estate but Lou barely gave it a glance. Then the owner drove him to his country club, where he played eighteen holes three times a week. He tried to invite Lou into the clubhouse for a drink, but Lou refused to get out of the car. "I haven't got time for games," he said.

The project went no further. When Lou returned to report to me, I asked him what happened. No matter how confrontational things get in our business, Lou almost always completes a project and leaves behind a happy and financially healthy client. He just shrugged and said, "Well, George, I guess he cared more about his status in the community than whether his business was failing. You know the type—another damn golfer."

A year later, we drove past the building where the business was located, but it was vacant. I'll take an educated guess that his business folded. Mr. Schwartz is going to have to find another way to pay his country club dues.

Many clients come around to our point of view about golf—if they're smart. We had a glass distributor as a client in New Hampshire three years ago that was in serious trouble. The company was just barely breaking even with $6 million in sales. They should have been netting between $400,000 and $800,000 a year. Instead, they were struggling to pay the bills. Things were so tight they couldn't afford accountants. They had to bring their wives in to do the bookkeeping. That's when you know you're in trouble.

Fore! (Closure, That Is)

Lou started the job on a Wednesday, and met with the two brothers who owned the second-generation business early that morning. They talked for about two hours. Then one of them stood up and said:

"Thanks, that was great. You're hired. See you tomorrow."

"Why, where are you going?" Lou asked.

"We have a golf tournament to go to. Tee off is in half an hour."

"Oh really? You have a business that is barely breaking even and you're going to play golf in the middle of the day? Good for you, but I won't be here when you get back."

The two brothers pleaded with Lou. They explained their father, the founder of the company, had just returned from a long trip and they were joining the tournament at his request.

"That's fantastic," Lou said. "Is he going to put $500,000 into the business?"

The father was getting a $100,000 annual stipend from the business, but he was retired. He spent most of his free time trying to lure his sons out to the country club during office hours. Lou was fuming. But the sons, who were in their thirties, seemed so sincere about wanting to fix things that he relented. Since they had paid to enter the tournament, he let them play nine holes, but told them if they weren't back by 3 p.m. the deal was off. They could find somebody else to clean up their mess.

At 3 p.m. on the dot they were back, with their father in tow. The three of them, along with Lou, stayed until 9 p.m. to make up for the hours they lost while they were honing their handicaps.

That was the last game of golf they played in the three months that Lou was on-site.

Obviously the problems in the company were more complicated than golf, but most of them stemmed the owners' eagerness to take off for hours during the workday when their business was limping along. The leadership was disengaged and distracted. By focusing their attention back on the business, monitoring cash flow, and being disciplined about cutting costs and maximizing efficiency, they turned the business around. Now the company's profit margins are a comfortable 8 percent. They've shored up losses and now net $500,000 a year in pure profits.

An addiction to golf is one of my first clues that a business owner needs a swift kick in the rear.

About five years ago we had a client—lets call him "Frank"—who lived in Queens, New York and sold and installed new and used office furniture. Frank was a great salesman. He generated about 70 percent of his company's revenue, and because of him it had grown into a small and profitable business. But then he started relaxing. He figured he deserved a break after working so hard. He took up golf.

He handed the reins over to his sales manager so his responsibilities wouldn't interfere with his swing. But his business soon landed in a sand trap. The sales manager was the worst possible choice for the job. He never left the facility, believing that he could move product simply by talking on the phone, and sales quickly dropped to the point where the business was no longer breaking even.

Frank ordered his sales manager to bring the sales back up. The sales manager's solution was to authorize the sales force to offer huge discounts to make the volume numbers look good, but it nearly bankrupted the company.

If Frank had bothered to micromanage the sales team like he should have, and demanded they run any discounts by him for approval, things wouldn't have reached that crisis point. But he was too busy working on his slice.

Money Doesn't Care How Warm and Fuzzy You Feel

In my experience, no matter what industry you work in, golf requires a huge expenditure of a business owner's time with little return on investment. Company retreats, seminars (except for mine, of course), and executive coaching classes can be just as bad as taking off a Tuesday afternoon for eighteen holes.

Consider the case of two brothers in New Jersey who owned a profitable business making custom stairwells and cabinets. The company lost money soon after they started going to Tony Robbins' motivational seminars. The business owners would spend $50,000 a year going to see him. It was like they'd joined a cult, and they expected their employees to pony up and find divine inspiration as well. There was no accountability and nothing was getting done. Half the staff was wandering around that place glassy-eyed, spouting Robbins' so-called wisdom. But walking on hot coals, eating more fish, and dreaming big doesn't build profits. What good is a pricey pep talk if you're not willing to show up and put in the work?

The partners didn't see this lunacy. They were in love with this feel-good guru. They'd spend thousands just to sit next to him on a private plane and watch him eat lunch. It got to the point where having a conversation with these guys was like hearing little girls talk about their pop star idols. It made me uncomfortable just listening.

While we were working with them, they wanted to interrupt the project to take their staff on a four-day retreat to Robbins' private island in the South Pacific. We could not get them to change their minds. They were convinced Tony Robbins was the reason for their success. But it was clear to us their obsession had started to affect their ability to run the business. So when they came back from the seminar, giddy and enlightened, we decided it was time to put their newfound philosophy to a challenge.

We told them to write down ten things they got out of it, and what they did with it. Of course, they said it was great. But when we asked them to tell us how the information could be applied to their business, they stuttered, stammered, and scratched their heads.

Of course they did. Because there was no substance to grab onto. It was just fluff. And while they were wasting their time on these empty platitudes, their business was going down the drain.

When you are off-site, you are not focused or setting priorities. That's what causes people to fail. A retreat is just a feel-good gesture in which everyone spends a day or two talking about the future and what they're going to get done—which of course never happens. It's another excuse not to work. Think about it. When you are on a retreat during the week, who's there to answer the phone?

If you feel the need for a company planning retreat, hold it in your back office after-hours on a weekday, but don't leave the building. Don't be like AIG. What do you think the $440,000 they blew on a corporate retreat to the St. Regis beach resort in California accomplished, besides a few nice tans, and maybe a massage or two, for their executives? Not that it matters, since it came out of the taxpayer's pocket in the form of a *$173 billion bailout*. They certainly weren't spending their own cash. They didn't have any!

But you, the small business owner, are a better breed. You built your business on your own back, not some government handouts. You don't have thousands of dollars and hours of free time to fritter away on useless perks and distractions.

Instead, get back to the office. Stay with your people. Micromanage and exercise your leadership skills. There's money to be made.

Give Up Golf

It's a waste of time. So are conventions,
trade shows, planning retreats . . .

■

No real business gets done at a trade show.
It's just a flimsy excuse for a paid vacation.

■

Let your competition play golf while you stay in the office
stealing their customers.

■

If you must play golf, do it after-hours. But you'll be better off
putting your country club dues back into the business.

■

Be wary of any activity that takes you and your employees away
from work. Payroll is too expensive to squander on useless activities.

■

And for God's sake, skip the motivational seminars!
Money doesn't care how warm and fuzzy you feel.

Teamwork Is Vastly Overrated

WHAT I AM ABOUT to say runs counter to what you will read in just about every other business book, but it's true:

Teamwork simply *doesn't* work in most businesses.

At least not in small and midsized businesses. Unless a company is profitable and disciplined, deferring your job to your team produces nothing but mediocrity and failure.

While I can see the argument for teamwork when it comes to large, well-established companies, in my many years of working with small businesses, I've found that insisting on teamwork is a fast route to lousy financial performance. Why? Because your team is only as strong as its weakest link. And while large corporations can afford a weak link here or there, small businesses just don't have enough room, or working capital, for that kind of failure. To be a successful small business owner, you must create an environment where the strong excel and the weak get fired.

If your sales manager isn't making his or her sales target, your whole team will suffer from that person's underperformance. If your production manager can't get the product out in time to meet your requests, you lose profits. If your accounting manager fails to give good financial guidance and transparent reporting, the sales and production managers will find themselves lost in the cosmos. A single lousy performance brings everybody down.

Let me be clear: A team is not to be confused with a department. Of course every small business, particularly the larger ones with fifty or one hundred employees, needs to be structured into different sections according to their various functions. But scrap the term *team* and all its incumbent baggage. Each department should have its own head and group of employees who work together to get things done, but there must be a clear chain of command. Those employees report directly to their department heads, and those department heads answer to you. Think of your employees as your army. Each one of them has a rank, and you are the general.

Ultimately, it's up to you to hold all of them accountable. I already wrote how you can set up a system of metrics that will hold everyone's feet to the fire. But the purpose of this chapter is to disabuse you of the false and widespread notion that your employees are your team, and you're all in it together.

Entire consultancies have been built on the premise that team-building is key to successful management and business survival. These so-called experts tell their clients to foster trust among their associates. Their books devote pages and pages to the various ways bosses need to pander to their employees and allow them to feel like they are all partners with an equal stake in the business. Over and over again, you hear the clichés: "There is no 'I' in team," "You have to let your team members experience believable communication," or "You have to motivate your associates and allow them to develop and grow." But you're not in the business of helping your employees "grow." To hell with that. Let them attend a Tony Robbins seminar on their own time if they feel the need for extra nurturing. During office hours the only growth they should care about is the growth of your profits.

When business owners expend their energy on office group hugs and retreats they can count on declining profits and productivity. Your employees are not associates—they are subordinates. You should also ban the use of the term *associates*. It blurs boundaries and allows your staff to forget that they are answerable to you, and ONLY you. You are paying them to perform a task and adhere to a business plan. Unless workers invest their own six-figures into the business, their only stake in your company is making sure they meet or exceed your expectations so they can continue to collect a paycheck. Trust is beside the point. It's a business, not a commune. The only thing your employees have to trust in is that you will be tough but fair, and that if they don't carry out the tasks you assign them, there will be consequences.

Yes, various colleagues and department heads have to collaborate, communicate, and coordinate to execute a plan. *But it's the business owner's job to lead that team and those people.*

Insist that each member perform individually. Place set goals and demands on each head, one by one. Have them report to you directly. Pump them up and kick their fannies. They have to know that at the end of the day they answer to you, not to each other.

There's a psychology at play here that the business school professional types who advocate teamwork often miss. If you put people together to work on an assignment, with no one left in charge and held accountable, you'll soon find out that no one wants to criticize their fellow team members. It's human nature. They feel secure in their mutual mediocrity. When the time comes to question or measure performance, no one wants to hear it. No one wants to be faulted. You assign them a task, and most of their time is going to be spent covering their behinds, and each others'. The minute the clock strikes five, watch how fast they disappear. And if the job isn't finished, you can bet the "team" won't show up on weekends to wrap it up.

Wings and Beer for the Team

Three years ago we started a project with a Ford dealership in Kentucky that was deep in the red. The losses were coming from the service and parts departments. Not surprisingly, the resulting lousy reputation for service at the dealership was hurting car sales.

The owner and his two sons had allowed their "team" to decide that the hours of the service would be from 8 a.m. to 5 p.m., Monday to Friday (in other words, when most people are at work). These geniuses ensured shorter working hours and less responsibility for themselves, while the Ford drivers in the area took their business elsewhere. Who wants to cut into their office hours to service their car? How many Ford owners do you know who can afford chauffeurs to run these errands for them?

It was clear what we had to do, but it would be drastic. Luckily, the dealership's owner was about to go on a three-week vacation to Florida. Before he left we made a deal with him to give us *carte blanche*. If he loved everything we did for him, he could pay us in full. If not, he could pay us for the two weeks work and we'd pack up our bags and leave.

We fired the service and parts managers. The owner was ridiculous for allowing this "team" so much latitude, and the fault lay at his feet. But these guys didn't deserve to remain employed. They didn't care whether the dealership made money, and whatever energy they had on the job was dedicated to finding ways to do as little work as possible and covering for each other. There was a sports bar down the street that saw more of these guys than any customer did. Why should the team care about sales when cold beers and a heaping plate of suicide chicken wings were waiting for them?

Next, we put the two with the greatest incentive to make the business work—the owner's sons—in charge of service and parts. As you know, I'm leery about family members having too much control, but these two were competent and more than willing to take on the extra responsibility. That's because they had some real skin in the game, since they were expecting to take over the business as soon as their dad retired. They agreed to extend service center hours from 7 a.m. to 9 p.m. They even put banners up in the streets announcing the new times. Within days the service and parts department revenues were up 30 percent.

When the owner got back from Florida, we had his sons present the changes to their father. He was thrilled and we got our money. We got rid of the team and established a hierarchy that would lead by example. Who else is going to do that? The janitor? No! It's up to the ownership.

Business improved so much the dealership was sold last year for a mountain of money, right before the car business cratered. All it took was a little self-motivation and accountability, something only possible when owners take *ownership*. Under team rule, that never would have happened. Instead, the business would have slowly hemorrhaged into nothing.

No-Go Team

If you want to know how well a team is working, just take a look around your office on Friday at 5 o'clock. Or on weekends. If you see anyone, it's probably because you just caught a glimpse of yourself in the mirror.

Only the individual who answers to you and has a shot at a promotion or a bonus check will be there on Sunday to go over inventory with you.

Team meetings should be quick and informational, not motivational. When you hold them, set inconvenient times. Do them after 5 p.m., on Saturdays, or at 7 a.m., before the workday starts. That way the meeting won't run over and waste time that would be better spent making sales calls.

To hell with democracy. End the meeting sooner by putting it to a vote—yours. Why should your employees have equal input? When the time comes to ask the bank for a credit line, and they want your personal guarantee, ask how many members of the team want to step up and write you a check. None? I thought so.

Small businesses don't have time for poorly performing teams. That margin for failure is too great; with a smaller staff, there's more on the line. If you want profits, you need a strong leader (you) and a group of hard-working subordinates who do what you tell them. Pay them well for performing and penalize them for underperforming. They have to know their paycheck comes from doing what you say and doing it well.

There Is No "$" in Team

A few years ago, we worked with a client in New York City, the owner of a once-thriving bus distribution company, who had an alleged management team made up of five people. This "team" had allowed profits to deteriorate to such an extent that the business was weeks away from failure. It was clear the owner allowed his team to put him against the wall financially. He was losing several hundred thousand dollars a year.

But the team alone wasn't to blame. The boss had not done his job. He abdicated too much of his authority, causing his team to fritter away time, make its own decisions, and hold two-hour meetings that accomplished little else than what to order from the local delicatessen.

No clear-cut goals were set. There were no timelines for putting a plan into action. Each manager was way overpaid for a business that was in a decline—taking home a check of about $70,000 a year without producing. When it came time to interview the team, I had to track each one down. For a large company housed in a huge 15,000-square-foot building, it was next to impossible to find one person working. But even in smaller spaces, people who are not doing their job have a habit of making themselves invisible.

We saved them the trouble and made them vanish altogether. By our third week on-site, three of the five managers were terminated, and the two who remained were given financial incentives to work harder. Newly anxious to prove their worth to the boss and earn a bigger paycheck, they started doing their jobs—something that never could have occurred if they'd continued blending in with their less-than-mediocre teammates.

Today the business has a fully functioning staff of five managers and the business has doubled in size. Its bank debt is now almost zero. The owner is in control of his business. With no more teams, each department head is held accountable for results daily. And the owner has increased his income tenfold.

Any business takes on the personality of its leader. If it's floundering, the owner is not doing his or her job and the "team" is falling into the vacuum created by a lack of leadership. If the boss wanders and procrastinates, the team will, too.

And here's a little secret: Most employees *want* strong leadership. They *crave* discipline. All the conventional wisdom about teamwork might sound appealing with its lofty idealism, but deep down people want clear structure and hierarchy. They want to be told what to do. They want to *know* where they stand.

A Mighty Mess

People are most comfortable when they understand exactly what is expected of them. But too few small business leaders are clear about what is wanted and expected of their staff. That's why a team of forty branch managers scattered across the country were so desperate for leadership by the time we started working with their CEO in 2004. This Virginia-based business that supplied audio visual equipment to trade shows—let's call it "Mighty Media"—was facing disaster. It was one of those rare cases when a business owner wanted us to skip the survey process and just get straight to work managing the operations. The company had just two months to liquidate all of its assets to repay its loans to the bank by the time we got the call. The terrorist attacks of September 11th devastated the trade show business, costing Mighty Media $20 million in lost contracts. Three years later they were still losing money. Between 2001 and 2004 the owner's net worth sunk to negative $3 million from $6 million. A company in business for more than thirty years—that once boasted $42 million in annual sales—was now broke.

Within forty-eight hours we were going to bat for Mighty Media with their bank. We won them a stay of execution, but only if the company would agree to a total restructuring.

Actually, that's an overstatement since there was no structure to this business at all! In forty-two years Mighty Media had grown to six hundred people scattered across the United States, and each branch office was an island unto itself. The COO, the CFO, and the president weren't offering any direction. The ownership referred to his branch managers as his team, but it was just another way of saying that no one had to answer to anyone. Each branch manager would get his or her $120,000-a-year salary regardless of profits. They saw the owner one day a year, if that. They weren't required to manage cash flow, travel costs, or payroll.

These branch managers operated on the assumption that, three months out of the year, during the convention season, they would be busy, and the rest of the year they would coast. With no accountability and little fear of the boss, no one understood they should be out there generating new business and tying expenses and cash flow to regional profits. They were ships at sea without a captain, and they were sinking fast.

We had every branch manager fly to Washington, D.C. for a company-wide meeting. We told them we were going to put a system of accountability in place and reduce the body count of each branch office by at least half. As soon as these employees understood the crisis the company was in, they were on board with the plan. You could almost hear the collective sigh of relief. Within three months of making these changes, the business was making $100,000 a month in net profit, after losing money for three successive years.

It wasn't the employees' fault the company was losing money; it was the owner's. His "team" was too geographically scattered and no one was connecting the dots. The CEO had poor financial controls, lousy communication skills, and, like many business owners, he assumed his management was omniscient when no one had a clue.

Step Up!

Passing things off to your team is just an avoidance tactic. The business owner can say to himself or herself, "Oh, my team is handling it." No. If your team isn't producing, *it's on you*.

The hardest thing for all business owners to do is look closely at their flaws. And if you refer to your employees as team members, you can bet no one will feel comfortable pointing out these weaknesses. It's far more comforting to be surrounded by a group of people who genuflect to the boss Monday through Friday than it is to establish authority and expect those who work for you to get their jobs done. That wouldn't happen in a company with a team culture, where employees duck and hide from accountability, finding safety in numbers. In these same businesses, incompetent bosses make themselves a part of the team, surrounding themselves with their top managers to avoid taking the reins and facing the truth.

But strong leaders know they are alone in this. That means you. If your business fails, you go with it. Let's be real. Your "team" won't suffer if you go under. They'll just go to work for the competition.

Forget Teamwork

A team is only as strong as its weakest link.

■

There is no "$" in team, just mediocrity and excuses.

■

Focus on individual performance.
Your employees are answerable to you, not to each other.

■

Team meetings should be quick and informational,
not motivational. Group hugs don't improve performance.

■

Employees crave strong leadership and structure.

■

Don't encourage diverse opinions. It's a business, not a democracy.

It's Not the Economy, Stupid, It's You!

THE WORST THING ABOUT a recession as severe as the current one is that it provides business owners an extra excuse for failure to perform their primary responsibility: making real profits.

If your sales are down, they'd probably be better if you'd followed the rules of this book earlier and implemented a tough, disciplined sales program. If your bank is pulling your line of credit and you can't find a new bank that will lend to your business, it's probably because you didn't make a profit last year and are still losing money this year. If your expenses are too high relative to your sales, you erred in not assuming the worst in your latest budget attempt. If your costs continue to be too high, then you haven't cut them mercilessly and without regard to family members, old friends, and underperforming employees.

If your sales are down 40 percent or 50 percent and you're continuing to lose money, you haven't adapted to the changing market realities.

If you're at the point where you're not able to realize modest profits and pay yourself, it's probably because the recent years of unparalleled national prosperity put you in a coma. You have a choice: Wake up or pull the plug.

Wudda, Cudda, Shudda

Now we're pushed against the wall and we can all look back over the past few years and see exactly where we lost huge amounts of profits.

Remember the automotive company from Chapter 11 that foolishly tried to pay all of its bills? We estimate the business could have saved at least $2 million by assiduously following our Profit Rules. The owners could have easily maintained a steady flow of payments to their vendors, and with better profitability would not have had their loan called by their bank. *Wudda, cudda, shudda* always makes it easier to excuse failure. But like we said earlier, that's not an option. Don't be a victim of circumstance. Financial failure was avoidable all along.

Remember the kitchen installation contractor in Northern Minnesota, also from Chapter 11? By the time I got his call, he was frantic. His sales had declined rapidly from $47 million to $6 million. His company had achieved $35 million in sales all at a loss.

It didn't have to be that way. Helped along by the boom in the housing market, the business had exploded from just $2 million five years ago. The owner bought houses, planes, cars, and boats—the whole deal. He was a self-made millionaire and damn proud of it. But over the last two years, his business started bleeding cash to the point where it was on life support.

The owner blamed the recession, but the buck stopped with him. The crash in the housing market merely exposed all the things he was doing wrong in the first place. Luckily he had been humbled just enough to open his ears and listen. The owner engaged us to help him set up a financial management system. What he needed was fiscal discipline. The toys and houses had to go, along with dozens of ineffectual employees. He closed three plants and downsized operations. The company still struggles at 10 percent of former revenue due to a dramatic housing downturn, but its financial prospects are improving. There is hope for it yet.

Hindsight tells him as well as us that he could have saved seven to ten points on those sales by closing factories earlier and getting rid of the unnecessary luxuries the business was affording him. The savings *cudda* easily equaled $8 million to $10 million. Instead of putting himself through a shredding machine leading to a Chapter 11 Reorganization, he *cudda* achieved more modest profitability and had a stable corporate environment and platform from which he could recover. This huge savings *cudda* propelled a real sales effort. He needn't have gone through the crushing personal blow of filing for bankruptcy.

It's Your Fault!

Sure, small business owners can blame the economy for their problems. Most people do. A faltering economy is a great excuse to throw in the towel, head for the golf course, and play the victim. But when you're making sales, especially sales in the seven-figure bracket, there is NO excuse for losing money! I don't care how bad the market is. This contractor's situation was a failure of leadership, pure and simple. He was too busy enjoying his new yacht to pay attention to his financials. He didn't have a clue what his overheads were; he had no financial reporting and therefore had no clue about his costs, or where he should cut to bring the business back into the black. He slipped into a comfortable state of denial and stayed there. He kept telling himself, "We'll get back this month's loss next month." As more time passed, he fell into even deeper debt.

It's a common mistake. But it's still inexcusable. Whether your enterprise is large or small, or you are operating in an economic boom or a recession, there should always be profits, and you should always be aware of what is on your balance sheet, and adjust costs accordingly.

But you still have to invest in your business. Stay in hiring mode. You should always be looking for good salespeople to go out in the field. Firing your sales department is the worst possible move at a time like this. You should be beefing up your team to counter what's going on. Most housing contractors had so much business they didn't need a sales department. Maybe they had one or two salespeople poking around, but they didn't have to try hard. Business came to them. But as business goes down, the contracting companies with a sales team could be picking up clients from the competition going under. Sure, practice effective day-to-day cash management. But keep up the sales push or watch sales plummet.

It's Up to You!

Don't be a victim. You don't have to be. As many times as we hear recession disaster stories, there are plenty of businesses following our rules and reaping healthy profits. We had a client in Reno, Nevada who put our rules in place and now enjoys quadruple sales and profits. The company, which retails and distributes mobility equipment for the disabled, such as stair lifts and electric wheelchairs, has a lock on a profitable niche market because of the strength of its sales and customer service team, and management's commitment to airtight fiscal discipline.

When we first worked with this small business ten years ago, the owner had two showrooms and $4 million in sales, but zero profits. Lack of cost controls and employee accountability meant the business was heading for a ditch. The owner, Don, was a great micromanager. The problem was he was trying to do everything himself. He had no effective management team in place. The team was so dysfunctional that to get something done he had to stay on top of each person. Each employee would yes him to death and never follow through on the commitment. One of the first things Don said to my consultant when we started the project was, "I can't get my people to do what I tell them to do." We hear this refrain over and over again from our clients. We had Don install a program that would hold people accountable and fire the non-performers. He called a meeting and drew a line in the sand.

"The train is pulling out of the station. You're welcome to come with us but you can step off now before we hit the rough part of the track," he told his staff. "You will face the possibility of being pushed off the train, but if the business does well and you make it, you'll be better by the end."

We helped him set up pay for performance, and those who stayed did well. With appropriate costing and budgeting systems in place, Don understood what he had to make based on his budgeting model and the actual cost of operations, and so did his remaining employees.

Meanwhile, Don's wife, who was in charge of customer service and sales, was underperforming. She felt she should be exempt from the new rules of accountability. The resulting tension was so bad that halfway through the project Don, just thirty-five years old, had to have open heart surgery. Don survived, and the unexpected crisis made him realize that in order to save himself and his business, he had to fire the missus.

Within five years the business grew from two show rooms to four, spread over multiple states. Today, sales are $8 million, and profits are soaring, even in this lousy economy. Sure, Don had to make a few adjustments. He made some cuts to payroll and laid off some people—tough decisions that were necessary to stay within the lines of his predetermined profit plan. Business has slowed down, but it is still robust. Because he followed all the rules, profits are not suffering nearly as badly as they are with so many other small businesses. And I am happy to report Don's health is good. The rules have become second nature and because of this, not only will he get through this recession, he will continue to flourish in good times and bad.

There is simply no excuse for failure. Like we tell all of our clients, if you want to follow the Profit Rules and be successful, it's your choice. Put these principles in action and make big money, or ignore everything we've presented here at your peril.

Grandpa George

At the turn of the last century my grandfather, who was also named George, walked across the Canadian border from Quebec into Maine with nothing but the clothing on his back and 25 cents in his pocket. He went on to found the first grocery store chain in the state and become one of its few millionaire residents.

When the Depression hit, he lost that business. But my grandfather was so determined to make money and provide for his family that he smelled an opportunity during Prohibition, and turned to bootlegging for his next money making venture. Of course, when Prohibition ended, he wound up destitute.

My father watched our family fortunes rise and fall like the Bay of

Fundy tide. When he graduated from college in 1932 he was ready to launch his career as an investment banker, but the markets crashed. He resolved to run for the beach and found himself a stable job in government, where he served as a career civil servant until he retired. He didn't trust the economy, the markets, or himself. He was afraid.

But I wasn't. Business was in my blood, and I couldn't escape the desire to go out into the world and make serious money. I loved the challenge of building something out of nothing. I caught the bug when I was at Harvard, working all the way through to pay my tuition and living expenses.

I started the first ski bus shuttle service between the Harvard campus and the ski resorts of the Berkshires—a venture that nearly got me thrown out of school. Before I graduated from Harvard Business School, I worked with Landlubber Jeans—the fashion company that started the worldwide craze for bell-bottom jeans in the early 1970s—helping the struggling business to turnaround. It was then I realized there are hundreds of measures any company can take to prevent losses and boost profits in good times and bad, if only they knew how. I even wrote my thesis on it!

As bad as the Depression was, I firmly believe there were things Grandpa George could have done to keep his grocery store chain alive. I wish I could have been there to help. I wish he could have had the benefit of my experience with small business owners just like him.

It's my mission to do for you what I could never do for my grandfather. It's too late for him, but it's not too late for you. There's still hope. The market might be tight, but if your business still has a pulse, you can pull yourself out of this trough. We've saved thousands of companies on the brink of disaster. Now it's time for you to save yourself.

Profits at Any Price!

Act now! Implement that sales plan and stick to it. Cut your costs and be ruthless about it. Use a scalpel, a hatchet, and a chain saw. Keep a tight lock on your cash flow. Comb through your profit and loss statements daily. Cut salaries and pay for performance. Follow a predetermined profit plan religiously. Forget sensitivity and teamwork. Give up golf. Fire unproductive family members. Pay a third of the invoice this week, and the other third next week. Drag it out as long as possible. Do all these things, every day, every year, in good times and in bad times.

Do all of the above, follow my Profit Rules, and I promise you'll sail through. When the tide turns, you'll be making the real money and you'll never have to worry about surviving another recession again.

It's Not the Economy, Stupid, It's You

Don't use the recession as an excuse. If you're not surviving it's because you weren't doing all that you should have during better times.

■

Resist the bunker mentality.
If you wait until the tide turns you will drown.

■

Take action. Cut costs, get aggressive about sales,
and fire mediocre workers.

■

Continue to invest in areas of your business that will generate growth,
like telemarketing.

■

Don't play the victim. As long as your business still has a pulse,
it's in your power to turn things around.

■

Follow my Profit Rules and you'll survive and thrive.

ACKNOWLEDGMENTS

I WOULD LIKE TO thank my loving and extremely supportive wife, Tiffany, who had to tolerate me as I wrote this book amidst the preparations for our New Year's Eve wedding in 2008. She also, incredibly, agreed to a six-month delay for the honeymoon. What devotion!

Chris and Lou Mosca, who have been working with me at American Management Services for over a decade, were invaluable in developing the content and sharing the anecdotes and client histories that are the meat of this book. Doug McDermod—another superb colleague who has been with us for twenty years and seen the inside of every airport in the country while carrying out his duties as director of management services—also carved out time from his hectic schedule to lend his enlightening perspective. And my sincerest thanks to the rest of our one hundred and fifty employees, without whose help this book would never have become a reality.

Special thanks to Samantha Marshall, who was invaluable in producing this book on a very condensed schedule and always made herself available to help, from whatever time zone she happened to be in, wherever she was in the world. Special thanks to Carol Mann, my devoted and brilliant agent who kept after me for months to do this book, for her experienced advice in putting this project together.

I'd like to thank the U.S. Conference of Mayors for their unwavering support, particularly Tom Cochran, Executive Director, and Mayor Dannel Malloy of Stamford, Connecticut, who has worked tirelessly on the PartnerAmerica program since its inception. Many of the past presidents of the U.S. Conference of Mayors provided incredible support and input into this project, including Mayor Manny Diaz of Miami; Mayor Donald Plusquellic of Akron, Ohio; Mayor Doug Palmer of Trenton, New Jersey; and former Mayor Wellington Webb of Denver, Colorado. A special mention of gratitude also to Current PartnerAmerica Task Force cochair, Columbia, Missouri, Mayor Darwin Hindman; former Kansas City mayor and PartnerAmerica Task Force cochair Kay Barnes; and all the mayors who have dedicated a part of everyday to America's small businesses. Thanks also to Kathryn Kretschmer-Weyland and Jeff Bean for their energy and insights.

ABOUT THE AUTHOR

DUBBED "THE TURNAROUND ACE" by *BusinessWeek*, George Cloutier brings more than thirty years of experience to his roles as founder and chairman of American Management Services—a consulting service that's widely considered to be the McKinsey of small business. He started the business in 1986, using just $42,000 in seed capital and steadily grew his tiny operation into a 150-plus employee operation with more than $20 million in annual revenue, with offices in Orlando, Florida; Boston, Massachusetts; and Washington, D.C. Cloutier also cofounded and serves as co-chairman of Partner America, a unique, public/private partnership between the U.S. Conference of Mayors and American Management Services dedicated to small business growth.

A cum laude graduate of Harvard College and Harvard Business School, Cloutier is well known as the nation's leading small business expert. In recognition for his dedication to small business, Cloutier was awarded the first-ever Small Business Advocate Award by the U.S. Conference of Mayors. The Minority Business Development Agency awarded Cloutier for being a critical partner in America's economic success. Cloutier was appointed to the Commerce Advisory Committee on Africa, by then-Secretary of Commerce

William M. Daley, to provide recommendations for creating a business environment in Africa.

His company also donated money to challenge business students and graduates to create a Peace Corps–style organization to assist small businesses in New Orleans after Hurricane Katrina. As a direct result of Cloutier's challenge, an existing organization was dramatically expanded and achieved multimillion-dollar funding. Dozens of businesses in the New Orleans area were also created or rebuilt. For his post-Katrina work, Cloutier was selected as Entrepreneur of the Year by Tulane University.

The nation's most outspoken advocate for the nation's 23 million small business owners, Cloutier has also been a vocal critic of the federal government's failure to adequately assist businesses on Main Street as it continually bails out major Wall Street banks and corporations with trillions of dollars in aid. Top economic and political professionals from around the world frequently solicit his advice on the issues faced by small and mid-cap companies. He's been invited to lead small business seminars and headline speaking engagements across the country, including major cities like Boston, Denver, Washington, D.C., Atlanta, and Miami. He has become a regular on national television programs such as *Fox Business News*, ABC's *20/20*, CNBC's *Squawk Box*, MSNBC, and Bloomberg Television. Cloutier is also a regular contributor and source to prestigious print publications, including the *Wall Street Journal*, the *New York Times*, the *Washington Post*, the *Washington Times*, the *Boston Herald, Inc.* magazine, *BusinessWeek*, *Fortune Small Business*, Reuters, the Associated Press, the Huffington Post, *Crain's New York Business*, the *Los Angeles Times*, Entrepreneur.com, msnmoney.com, cnnmoney.com, USNews.com, and *Forbes Small Business*.